LIFESCAPES

ALSO BY ANN WROE

LIFESCAPES

A BIOGRAPHER'S SEARCH
FOR THE SOUL

ANN WROE

W PUBLISHING GROUP

AN IMPRINT OF THOMAS NELSON

Published in Nashville, Tennessee, by W Publishing, an imprint of Thomas Nelson.

Thomas Nelson titles may be purchased in bulk for educational, business, fundraising, or sales promotional use. For information, please email SpecialMarkets@ThomasNelson.com.

Scripture quotation marked KJV is taken from the King James Bible. Public domain.

Any internet addresses, phone numbers, or company or product information printed in this book are offered as a resource and are not intended in any way to be or to imply an endorsement by Thomas Nelson, nor does Thomas Nelson vouch for the existence, content, or services of these sites, phone numbers, companies, or products beyond the life of this book.

ISBN 978-1-4003-4795-7 (audiobook)
ISBN 978-1-4003-4794-0 (ePub)
ISBN 978-1-4003-4793-3 (TP)

Library of Congress Control Number: 2024941537

Printed in the United States of America
24 25 26 27 28 LBC 5 4 3 2 1

Contents

Preface

IN 2009 I WROTE AN OBITUARY OF A FISH. IN MY twenty years of doing obituaries for the *Economist*, this marked a departure. But it was August, news was slow, and the weather was hot; so, sitting in my shed at the bottom of my north London garden, I imagined myself instead in the silty depths of a lake near Peterborough.

The fish was Benson, a carp—probably a she—who was, for time, the most famous fish in England. She weighed twenty-nine kilograms and had died, it seemed, from eating too many uncooked tiger nuts. She was a gourmand but also a paragon of loveliness. So it flowed on:

> In her glory days she reminded some of Marilyn Monroe, some of Raquel Welch. She was lither than either as she cruised through the water weed, a lazy twist of gold. Her gleaming scales, said one fan, were as perfect as if they had been painted on. . . . Her lips were full, sultry or sulking, her expression unblinking; she seldom smiled. Yet the

reeds held fond memories of her friend Hedges, her companion in slinky swimming until she, or he, was carried away in 1998 by the waters of the River Nene.

Abandoned, she ate more. Cubes of cheese, scraps of luncheon meat, bread crusts, Peperami, dog biscuits, and tutti-frutti balls all came down invitingly through the water. She sampled most of them. Of course, she was not fool enough to think they came from heaven. Carp are cunning, a very fox of the river, as Izaak Walton said. She could see the lines, and at the end of them the trembling shadows of Bert, or Mike, or Stan, spending an idle Sunday away from the wife with a brolly and a can of beer. Often she continued to lurk, roiling the mud to conceal herself and basking in her own scaled beauty, as carp will. On hot days she would rise to the surface, glowing and tantalising, with a lily-leaf shading her like a parasol. She played hard-to-get, or the One That Got Away, nudging the line before drifting down toward the dark serene. But then, just for the hell of it, she would take the bait.

The first hookings hurt horribly, the whole weight of her body tearing her tongue like a razor blade. But over the years she got used to it, and her leathery mouth would seize the bait as a prize. Hauled to the limelight, she was admirably unfazed. . . . She had her picture taken with Tony, owner of her lake, who confessed to the *Wall Street Journal* that he had "quite a rapport" with her; with Ray, who caught her at two in the morning, disturbing her beauty sleep; with Matt, of the shy smile and the woolly hat; and with Steve, who ungallantly told *Peterborough Today* that she felt like "a sack of potatoes" and was "available to everyone." She was not, but at least fifty people held her, or gripped her, for a moment or so. Uncomplainingly, she nestled in their arms before she was lowered to her element again.

It was news to me that fish could be caught and released so often: that, in the end, they might even let themselves be caught. It made me look differently at the anglers sitting with their tea-flasks and nylon bivouacs by the Hampstead ponds, just waiting for the weed-or-water ripple that might give their prey away. How much easier, I thought, than my job: trying to catch human lives, week after week, in one thousand words.

One day, I suppose, science will announce what life is and how it began—if it began. Until then I have been grappling with a mystery, perhaps the most fundamental of all: the nature of this force, which, as Shelley put it, our bodies "enshrine for a time." The word *enshrine* confirms that even for Shelley, who was no believer, it seemed ridiculous to think of life, that "astonishing thing," as merely physiological and mechanical. It seems equally absurd to me.

Instead, I think of my work as catching souls. It is the best word I know for the unique and essential part of ourselves, our self-conscious and transcendent core. I happen to believe in the soul as a concept. Many of my subjects did not, and I would never dream of foisting that belief on them. My surmises are my own. Nevertheless, it is soul that I go looking for. Or, to put it another way, real life.

Over the years I have tried many ways of ambushing life, in long form or short, from a quick haiku to doorstop biographies. All the attempted snares and traps come in for consideration here. Many of my conclusions I have drawn from my subjects; more from life itself, as it springs surprise after surprise. One thing is certain: from our point of view, life always gets away.

And then returns. And then returns.

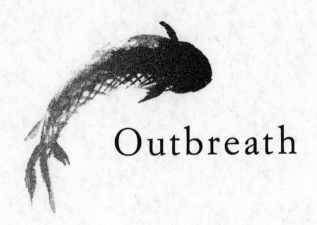

Outbreath

1. Possessing

THE VILLAGE WAS TRANQUIL FLINT-AND-BRICK, shaded by great trees. My friends and I had made a detour there to get a watch repaired. The house we needed stood at the bottom of a steeply rutted lane; just beyond the gate was a stand of jams and chutney for sale, with dewy bags of fresh watercress. It was mid-July, sunny and hot. The jovial watch-mender invited us to have tea outside, and we chatted for about an hour. But my attention wandered sometimes to another presence, almost invisible, silent, busy.

Before we saw her she had run away,
the little wife,
leaving a section of the watercress
in pale neat swards
among the rioting grass, blaze-dandelions,
   exultant birds—

Sun-dazzled greenhouse panes had hidden her,
bent with her knife

over the dancing, sparkling stream beneath
his swelling shirts—
now in the kitchen she shakes bunches out
under the spurts

of an ungovernable tap. Outside
we drink and laugh;
inside, past shelves of jam- and chutney-jars
washed, dried and shone,
she keeps her head bowed to the endless job
that must be done,

her silent life,
the little wife.

That poem was sheer presumption. All I knew of "the little wife" was a stainless-steel knife left in a watercress bed; a plastic washing line; an unruly tap; and shelf after shelf of empty, shining jars. All I saw of her was a dark, bent head and birdlike body, perhaps Malaysian. Yet from these few things a life seemed to form, and not a happy one. I heard years later that the watch-mender had died, leaving her nothing, and she had fled from the house and the village as if they were a prison. When I next passed the house, the watercress beds and the stand had gone. Instead there were footballs and a gaggle of ducks. My pursuit of lives often proceeds this way.

Chronologies, ancestries, and even achievements may reveal curiously little about a man or a woman. On the other hand, the smallest things may offer vital clues. A brass letter-opener, a much-mended cardigan, a favourite word—a line of jars—may catch them much more sharply. The more other people are brought in, with their own assessments and perspectives and their bland praise, the more the particular life escapes. It becomes a studio portrait where the subject stands stiffly against a backdrop of mountains or sea, with the photographer's own props on the table and a scrubbed expression, album-ready.

Life is far less formal. One friend of mine is best evoked by a tennis racket thrown on an unmade bed and an end of baguette studded with raw garlic, his favourite snack. Another, from primary school, is remembered by her leg brace, a box of thirty-two different crayons, and the dance of iron filings on a magnetised piece of paper—a wonder she showed me as we perched on the fire escape. Two maiden aunts are summed up in the immense privet hedge that towered outside their French windows, and in willow-pattern plates laid with slices of cold mutton. Hats are eloquent: the broad-brimmed bush-hat of a Zimbabwean friend, sported proudly in the Welsh rain; the snappy panama of a colleague in Virginia, worn with a seersucker suit that breathed the antebellum South; or the hard pillbox adopted by Great-Aunt Edye, complete with a veil as scratchy as herself. I like to think I am summed up in my favourite jacket, frayed away at buttonholes and elbows, collar and cuffs, because it smells of rain and the hills, and each bramble-snag records some scrape or other.

Handwriting seems a giveaway: a signature that shrinks into a corner, a bold Pentel scrawl, hungry descenders that grab the line below. But there is eloquence, too, in a favourite mug (Spurs, James Bond, an abstract print), the arrangement of tools (precise, graded, disordered), a pair of glasses (flamboyant, sober, or wire-rimmed, worn slightly askew, as if thrust on in a rage). When I think of yet another great-aunt, it is cake that catches her.

> With wrinkling mouth
> Aunt Fairy
> blows upon her tea,
> suspicious as a sheep
> that steps towards the hay
> heaped in a metal pen,
> pulls out a strand or three—
> but then shoves boldly in,
> with loose lips
> swallowing down before
> she tastes the Rich Fruit cake
> too briefly on her plate,
> and butts back in for more.

I might also have focused on her hanging-down stockings, or the slanting, wide-legged walk caused by her bad hip. But it was cake that caught her: one sort in particular, sprinkled with Demerara sugar and damp with boiled fruit. She spoke the very word as if she chewed and tasted it, with a half-laugh of relish that life could contain such delicious, succulent things.

When we left that café (in Brighton, decades ago, near the Pavilion) life clung to her teacup and plate and the disarranged cushion on her chair. It tends to do so. A glove dropped in the street still trembles and gesticulates with the presence of its owner, who was fumbling in a bag or distracted by some thought as the bus drew up. A Roman perfume bottle of tarnished blue-green glass evokes not only an eyebrow, a lip, a delicate wrist, but some woman's fantasies of beauty. A shoe, even from centuries ago, water-dark leather crushed out of shape, nonetheless preserves the weight of a foot and the care of fingers fastening. After modern disasters, when people run away, they tend to shed their footwear for greater speed. When the Israelis pursued the Egyptians in the rout that ended the Six-Day War in 1967, they came across a part of the desert littered with panicking shoes.

Another shoe, a trainer, lay for months on a half-roof in Gower Street in London. From the street you could not see it, so no one removed it. It looked like the tossed-away remnant of some fight between youngbloods, but it was small; it had belonged, perhaps, to a child of eight or nine. It was not high-fashion, as the fashion was then: cut too low on the ankle, too thin on the tongue, and without a showy button to inflate it. But it looked new, with smart diagonal flashes on the uppers and the regulation trailing laces. Some boy would have put it on each morning, struggling over the knots, perhaps late for school or being urged on by friends on bicycles; he would have felt a sense of achievement as he tightened the loops, standing a bit straighter afterwards. Some careworn mother, too (ghost hovering beside ghost), would have been pestered to make this purchase, now gone for nothing. The discarded trainer still sang of all this: pride, sacrifice, waste. On Brighton beach far scruffier fragments lie among the pebbles. Just litter, you could say: scraps not yet harvested by the man who wanders among the deckchairs with a grabber and a black bag, moving to the sounds of old Motown from the waking-up pier. Each fragment is sea-rubbed, insignificant, but each suggests a life. That unravelling piece of green nylon rope came from a fishing boat, probably attached to a lobster creel, perhaps lost overboard on some day when the sea blew up rough and winds were lashing the skipper in his soaked, slick rubber overalls. His frustration is in it. That blue cap came from a sunblock bottle shaken by a pony-tailed girl over shoulders already too plump and pink, which would be really sore the next day, but she didn't care. That fifty-pence piece, dull with salt and air, was part of a small girl's ice-cream money, whose loss she wept over with hot tears while her mother scolded her. (It reminds me of another coin, darker and far older, picked up among the weeds in the Circus Maximus in Rome: a *quadrans* of Nerva dropped, as I instantly imagined, by a slave going for bread, desperately feeling in his tunic for it, tensing for a whipping.) Even the stones, when I pick them up, carry the grooves of past collisions and the movement of old fire.

Beyond them the sea sighs in and out, eroding, disposing: in Paul Valéry's words, *"toujours recommencée,"* always starting again.

Pontius Pilate, whose life I wrote, had to be caught from pieces not much larger than these. Gospels and histories record certain deeds, even some alleged words, of the Roman governor who crucified Christ. But of the man almost nothing is known. The volume of Tacitus has gone that might have mentioned him. His daily reports to Rome (the tedious duty of all governors) have disappeared. His career before Judaea is a mystery. The hard evidence that remains is a handful of coins and a broken dedication stone.

I bought myself one of Pilate's coins for Christmas, from a shop opposite the British Museum. It is a *prutah* from the year of the crucifixion, the second-smallest of the coins he minted in Judaea; it might have bought a handful of figs. It is bronze, now turned dark green, thin with age and wear. The symbols are ones he would have chosen: on the obverse, a *lituus* or augur's staff, a sign of "superior" Roman religion and Roman good fortune; on the reverse, a victorious, fruitful laurel branch. On both symbols the bright coppery bronze still gleams in places through the patina, giving them just the effect Pilate wanted them to have. This little bit of power and propaganda was all his own, and as close as we can get to the life of him. But the dedication stone, too, tells some of his story: that he described himself not as an administrator but as a *praefectus*, a mounted military man.

From these hints, and from common Roman things, I tried to build him up: the inauspicious days marked in red on his calendar, the faint whiff of shellfish dye in his toga, his homesickness for news-sheets and fried snacks seized from a street-stall, his joy in chariot-racing (*Go, Greens!* or *Go, Blues!*), his mouth-freshening pastilles in the morning; his superstitions, as a man who took auguries, about birds, storms, left-handedness, a trip on a step. I boldly surmised that he might have shared the Roman taste for the strange luminescence of decaying things, and for the colour of dried blood. A sort of hologram would form then, an invented existence. Yet I did not even know his *praenomen*, the name his mother or his lovers had called him by, whether *Marcus* or *Lucius* or *Quintus*: the breath that warmed him and roused him and to which he answered, his real life.

My task was scarcely easier with Perkin Warbeck, who posed as (and just possibly was) one of the missing fifteenth-century princes in the Tower. There was one authentic portrait, though sketched much later from a painting, and uncertain faces stitched in tapestries; there were scraps of handwriting, and brief assessments by other people. Yet this was a young man with at least two alternative histories, two accounts of himself, and a multiplicity of names, depending on who was observing him. Somehow, one life united them. It glimmered perhaps in his dandified love of gold chains and particoloured hose, in a certain talent for keyboard music, his fits of proud petulance and his dread of battle, in whatever persona he was. I looked at the portrait for hours, trying to read him, with his pretty mouth and strangely lustreless left eye, which offered no communication. In the British Library I sat with a letter of his from October 1496, written by a secretary but signed by the Pretender with such flowing eagerness that he had to crowd the last few letters clumsily together. What did that show? Hard to tell. All I knew was that a thrill, like a caught breath, still came from the brown ink, the thick rag paper, and the thought that his hand and wrist (probably sleeved in cloth of gold) had moved across the paper where, surreptitiously, I moved mine after him.

Such fragments had to do. They were like small dabs of paint applied to a canvas, heightening here, contrasting there, adding colour, to try to make life spring out. In another book the experiences of fourteenth-century towns-folk could be drawn closer in the guttering of a candle, the greasy pile of a fleece, the lather flecking a messenger's horse, the tang of sealing wax. As I burrowed into the municipal documents of Rodez, in south-central France, I wandered through a neglected allotment (the subject of a tax dispute), brushing thistles and treading down brambles; felt the blushes of a girl harassed as she sold pears in the market, and the callous clumsiness of the youth who seized one and said they were bad anyway; heard a local sergeant, hampered by his rod of office, cursing and tumbling downstairs. Such details telescoped time until these distant figures seemed to jostle round me, chattering in the twangy Occitan that was still spoken in the streets outside.

In the registers of town accounts, the medieval treasurer (whose sketched hand, in the margins, would point out various names as "idiots" or "whores") marked his place with long straws plucked from the floor. He put several in the pages for 1348, when the Black Death had carried away perhaps one-third of the town's taxpayers. As I read the litany of *mort es*, *mort es*, *mort es*, I felt half-afraid to touch the straws, in case the bacillus still crawled in them. I remember how quiet the library seemed then, with the elegant attendant yawning at her watch and the plump man to my left picking his teeth over the *Dépêche du Midi*, as the register seemed to tremble in hands other than mine.

Such books are still warm with life. In the London Library, some are too much so. Who was the eccentric, for example, who scribbled all through the *Selected Letters* of Edward Thomas—his underlinings, wiggles, crosses, and ticks? Or wrote out again in the margin the words that had struck him, such as *ghyll*, *firelighter*, and *haversack*? Sometimes he would write "Yes!" and circle it. He was neat, at least; he used a fine, sharp pencil. I could picture him, young, male (his obsessiveness suggested that), thin, and particular, long-fingered and long-nosed. I could see him riffling through index cards, and feeling for a handkerchief in the pocket of a tweed jacket much like the ones Thomas wore. All through the book he muttered and exclaimed away, with the occasional loud sniff.

Other books ring with old debates. Shelley loved to argue in his marginalia, in pencil that gets blacker and blunter as he goes on, sprawling sometimes across two pages to show the extent of his scorn. He lives again in every one. Various ancient books that I have found in the London Library, surprisingly on the open shelves, leather-bound and with a typeface as bold as Caxton's, have more querulous marginalia, usually in ink. The pages are often stained with wine or candle wax. Immediately I see a man sitting up late in a dark study, huddled in a dressing gown and possibly a nightcap, bent close to the page to read with thick-lensed glasses. Or I am part of an argument between full-wigged scholars in a coffeehouse, the book open on the table and shoved from hand to hand, like a dangerous thing: a live thing.

In the weekly round of obituaries, too, life catches on possessions. The whole existence of Naty Revuelta, the mistress of Fidel Castro, seemed to lie in two houses and their furnishings. The first was a big, beautiful villa in Vedado, the most elegant part of Havana, where the shutters opened each morning on the white scent of jasmine. This was the moment when her baby, Alina, would be taken away by the nurse to be fussed and dressed in lace. In the late afternoons, after an unsleeping siesta, her sparkling company might be sought for tennis and canasta parties. Most of the rest of her marriage was spent in darkness in this house, watching television until the moment when her husband, Orlando, a cardiologist, came home and fell asleep in his chair.

Yet once she had decided to let Fidel "indoctrinate" her—the word having, for him, no baser meaning—she sent him the front-door key. It was sealed in a linen envelope lightly scented with Lanvin's Arpège, and after five in the afternoon, on most days, he and two henchmen would come to sit among her imitation French furniture and fine English tea sets, plotting revolution. Her dressing-table drawer held plush cases of jewellery set with diamonds, emeralds, and sapphires, and certificates of her savings; she sold them all for Fidel's cause. He could buy rifles with that money, even if social convention stopped her fighting beside him in the mountains: kept her, for the most part, imprisoned in that impressive house.

The second house she lived in, in Nuevo Vedado, was smaller and uglier. Naty moved there when her marriage ended and Fidel, on the arm of a different woman, had ascended to power. This house, too, was often in darkness behind heavy metal grilles, like those which in nineteenth-century Spain enclosed the young women of the family. Here the shutters kept out robbers. The walls were built of breezeblocks, painted cream, but portraits of her past self in high society still covered both them and the sideboards. One drawer held the ration book with which, like most Cubans, she qualified for her share of black beans and rice and queued patiently to get them; yet they were served to her by her one remaining maid, Chucha, on a silver tray. She smoked long cigarettes from a gold case and sipped her strong black coffee from tiny gold-rimmed cups, the sort without handles, held lightly between thumb and fingers. And almost daily, from her lingerie drawer, she would bring out the bundle of love letters Fidel had written to her. She kept them in a blue satin case, tied with a blue silk ribbon; one by one, she slowly unfolded them. Those letters held her lover's weight and purpose, as well as the warm musk smell of his cigars. She would read them aloud as she sat alone. In my mind she was like a figure from the novels of Gabriel García Márquez, stilled in her chair amid vivid incongruities, like the rebels who cradled her delicate flowered china on laps that bulged with pistols and bandoliers. She sat, too, as in one of his claustrophobic interiors, against a wall of slatted sunlight and beneath a fan that hardly moved the humid air.

Many miles to the north, Bobby Fischer's life was caught on chessboards. His mother tried to cure him, consulting psychologists and the columns of the Brooklyn newspapers, but still she could not stop the pocket set coming out at the dinner table. As a boy, he skipped school to spend his mornings in the dingy cabinet room of the Marshall Chess Club in Manhattan, reading through the file cards of nineteenth-century games. In a particular seat at the New York Public Library, he sat for hours immersed in chess history. In the family's walk-up flat, once his mother and sister had moved out, he set up continuous chess games beside each bed, ignoring the outside sunshine to compete against himself.

If you could see inside his brain, as rivals hoped to, you would find it primed to attack and defend in every way possible, with a straight-moving rook or a sidling bishop, or with both in his favourite Ruy López opening, or with the queen swallowing an early pawn in the "poisoned" version of the Sicilian, or a thousand others. Chess, he once said, was life, and there was nothing more. He had never done anything else, had not persevered in school, was no good at any other subject; he had pinned every watchful minute of his existence to thirty-two pieces and sixty-four black-and-white squares. He reminded me, as I wrote, of a bird of prey hovering, ready after long thought to dart and spring: a bird solitary, perched on a chair as on a fence post, focused on nothing but the territory before him. He dreamed of a house in Beverly Hills that would be built in the shape of a rook.

As Fischer brooded, his fingers laced like claws across his forehead to keep ruses in and enemies out, elsewhere in Manhattan a typewriter-mender sat at his trade in his upstairs repair shop in Fulton Street. Martin Tytell was surrounded by new, wet Mylar ribbons, shiny chrome levers, and pieces of type, for the typewriter in all its forms and parts composed his life. His ear was tuned to the chatter and *ping!* of broken Remingtons and Smith Coronas, to whom (not "which," for they had souls) he offered psychoanalysis in a notice on his door. He could cure any of them, "whether . . . frustrated, inhibited, schizoid, or what have you," treating them as tenderly as though they were human beings; for the platen around which the paper was wound, hard and dry or plump and soft, was, he said, a typewriter's heart. After a brief while of peering with screwdriver in hand, he could tell exactly when they had left the factory, how they had been treated and with what pressure, timid or furious, their owner had hit the keys. He then set carefully to work, natty in bow tie and with a pipe clamped in his mouth, to mend them or re-engineer them to speak in different tongues, characters, and notations, before leaving the convalescents to sleep in their plastic shrouds.

When his shop closed in 2001, after sixty-five years, it held a stock of two million pieces of type. The letters *n* with a tilde, all by themselves, took up a whole shelf. In one dark nest of metal cabinets dwelled a full drawer of umlauts. Each typewriter was, to him, an individual; its spark did not come through a cable in the wall but lay within. It showed in each distinguishing mark—that sluggishness in the type-bars, that particular wear on the *s*—that would be left, like a fingerprint, on the paper. Those many machine-lives merged with his.

Much of my time is spent searching for such details. Leona Helmsley, sharp-tongued queen of New York hotels, carrying her Maltese called Trouble in her handbag; Osama bin Laden's love of sunflowers, and his habit of riding through the woods on Fridays on a white horse, in imitation of the Prophet; the red Gucci slippers worn by Benedict XVI under his austere white robes. Many are surprises, such as the playwright Arthur Miller's lifelong delight in making things with wood. At fourteen, he saved up to build a back porch on the family house; in old age he made tables, chairs, a bed, and a cabinet, exactly planed and balanced. To make

14

extra-sure the angles were right, he once consulted a mathematician. Reading *The Brothers Karamazov*, he was amazed by Dostoevsky's description of precisely how a window was hinged. Miller the carpenter was speaking then, his life concentrated in rule, frame, and spirit-level, as well as in the making of perfectly calibrated plays.

Master-biographers have long shown how life resides in details. In the seventeenth century John Aubrey took pains to note that Thomas Bushell, servant to Francis Bacon, wore "more buttons than usuall" on his cloak; that Bacon himself would have his table strewn with "Sweet Herbes and Flowers" at every season, to refresh his spirits; that Thomas Hobbes would draw lines on his thighs and on the sheets in bed, to do mathematical calculations; and that James Harrington, a political theorist, had a fantasy that his perspiration turned into flies and bees, which he would prove by sitting in a timber shed on hot days until flies crept out of their lurking holes. William Oughtred, a mathematician, lived in poverty but entertained royally the academics who visited him, receiving them in "an old red russet cloak-cassock that had been black in dayes of yore, girt with an old leather girdle." In case inspiration came in the small hours, he kept his tinderbox by him, and an inkhorn fixed on top of his nightstand. We do not see Oughtred in dry equations, though his mind swarmed with them; we see him shabby, inky, struggling to get a light, living.

Suetonius did the same for the Caesars, never fearing to digress from their political and military careers for some impertinent, pertinent detail. Augustus, he wrote, liked boxing not merely between professionals, but between ruffians slugging in city alleys; he hated to be called "My Lord," and his metaphor for swift action was "quicker than boiled asparagus." This suggested a man who haunted kitchens, as well as marble halls. Tiberius, who disliked waste, would serve half-eaten dishes at his formal dinners, and so prided himself on his knowledge of Greek literature that he would quiz professors on, for example, exactly what song the Sirens sang. Claudius was so absent-minded that he would send for men to play dice with, forgetting that he had already had them killed. The very randomness of these traits made Suetonius's subjects even more terrifying. They became symbols of the unpredictability of fate and of the world, in the throw of a die or the landing of a punch.

Often, as the details accumulate, I take on my subjects' obsessions. As I wrote about David Esterly, a wood-carver, I could feel the heft of the different tools in my own hand and the character of different woods, as he described them, under the blade: the buttery softness, almost oiliness, of limewood, the hardness of ash, the sluggishness of beech. Esterly imitated with wonderful skill the *trompe l'oeil* technique of Grinling Gibbons, a seventeenth-century genius of the form, carving in limewood with a gouge held like a pencil, drastically undercutting until the wood was scarcely thicker than a petal and the piece filled with shadow and air. Following him, I understood wood and the working of it in new ways, even if that expertise was a millimetre thick and eventually, inevitably, fell away like a smooth-planed shaving to the floor.

Writing of Leon Fleisher, a pianist who lost the use of his right hand, I began to experience his terror of paralysis, the exercises and bindings that did not help, the horror of fumbles and disappearing skill. The black-and-white keys, formerly his playground, were now resisting him. Fleisher gradually realised, as his hand seized up, how the fourth and fifth fingers of that hand were essential to the playing of trills, especially the ascending ones in the cadenza of the adagio of Brahms's First Piano Concerto, his favourite piece. When he prolonged those trills just a little, with a touch of the pedal, he could produce a resonance like the shimmering of the universe. In imagination I pressed the pedal after him, setting the stars trembling; all through writing the piece I felt my own fingers stiffening, curling under, putting that resonance beyond both him and me. Yet he eventually learned to view his hands differently, as equals in dexterity and potential. He had always thought of his right hand as the singer, doing most of the important work; but he discovered that the left hand, even by itself, gave him more to say at the piano, providing both harmony and rhythm, like a heartbeat. That became a lesson for me, a mere listener, as well as for him.

With Hunter S. Thompson, the doctor of gonzo journalism, I dwelled with his own grim delight on the firepower that lay around his farm in Woody Creek: .44 Magnums, 12-gauge shotguns, black snub-nosed Colt Pythons with bevelled cylinders, .22-calibre mounted machine guns. He also kept explosives, to blow the legs off pool tables or to pack in a barrel for target practice. Day by day, he tended to have a rifle in his hand. And after the armaments he stashed up drugs, obtained for the desert crossing in 1971 that inspired *Fear and Loathing in Las Vegas*: "Two bags of grass, seventy-five pellets of mescaline, five sheets of high-powered blotter acid, a salt shaker half-full of cocaine, and a whole galaxy of multi-colored uppers." This cocktail began to take hold, he wrote, "somewhere around Barstow." I, too, had driven in the Californian desert, and pictured Thompson's rattling Chevrolet Caprice in the scene I saw as we descended towards Palm Springs from the San Bernardino Mountains: an empty highway stretching to infinity and on it a single patrolman stopping a single car, presumably for speeding.

Gentler spirits also drew me into their worlds. With Agitu Gudeta, a peasant cheese-maker in Italy, I stirred the great vats of curds and felt a special pride in her treasures, the small fresh-salted cheeses that, in a few days, would taste completely different. I sampled, too, the herbs the goats were feeding on, rosemary, marjoram, and sage flavouring their blue-white milk; stroked their fine piebald hair as she did and pressed my cheek to their high curving horns; cleaned the muck and mud from their udders; and scoured the milking buckets until they shone. With Barry Lopez, who studied man's relationship with landscape, I walked across the Arctic tundra, possessing it detail by detail. Like him, I bowed to the horned lark as she sat unblinking on her nest, and to the golden-plover eggs, touched with a glow as soft as dawn light; I bowed to a shred of musk-ox hair caught in the lavender flowers of saxifrage, to the cobalt melt ponds in the far distance, and (visible only through binoculars) the bloom of glittering spray around caribou as they shook themselves after bathing. Nature deserved to be honoured in this way.

As the props accumulate, they can create a portrait of

unexpected consequence. My subjects seem to become archetypes, representing whole aspects of life; they stand for more than they are. It is a transformation especially conferred by poetry, when it rests for a moment on one figure in a scene. Pinned down in a poem, "the little wife" became for me a symbol of all women trapped in loveless, exploitative marriages; and a local shoe-mender became an exemplar of all men whose hopes for their business have faded with ill-health or middle age.

> The "Hard-Working Cobbler"
> never had enough to do—
> put on weight, grew puffy, sat
> becalmed among his lasts as slow
> packed buses lumbered by.
> His straps were pretty good,
> long-wearing. Those of Time
> squeezed tighter than they should.

A woman at a Cotswolds drinks party, standing a little apart and less elegant than the rest, could be seen as a typical victim of the British class system, judged and silently dismissed.

> She wears blue silk,
> has a peacock feather
> stuck in her hair,
> shows off the dirt
> under half-painted nails;
> it belongs there.

She trims the lawns
at the PM's country seat,
down on her knees silent with shears
close-clipping in the shade
of lordly trees,

while past the wall
and from the avenue
where statues brood,
she hears the cut-glass din
of parties she's not in,
the great, the good.

Other people, though, became consequential because they
were suddenly transfigured, as though by rays of the sun.

At Euston underpass he waits to cross—
felt hat, grey mac, a broad uncertain face.
"Plotkin, magician" is the name, embossed in
black Cyrillic on his small tin case.

I once observed another one like him
sitting alone in Scarborough, some old lag
feeding the birds; with, in its garish trim,
"Home Magic" poking from a plastic bag.

You might dismiss them with no second thought,
end-of-the-pier acts, amiable fools.
But I saw violets spring round Plotkin's feet,
and, from "Home Magic," jewels.

Fifty and simple, thin grey hair
held with a sparkly slide,
she has picked the red valerian
that somehow grew beside
the dustbins; holds it now
radiant with smiles and pride
as any flowering bride.

Beauty in everyday, as when
a worn-out woman, cigarette
lodged unlit on her lower lip
gives her white roses, "Fiver for
the bunch in Asda," to a man
who's waiting only for the bus—
and so to every one of us.

After a death, relatives sort through the personal effects and
take, as mementoes, this and that. They do not need much.
Clothes are thrust into black bags, or taken to the charity
shop, with a sort of horror; the weight and wear of the body,
the brown ring at the shirt-collar, the sour persistence of old
perfume, are life brought too close. Soft furnishings, too,
may know altogether too much.

The old chair thrown out by the council wall,
green padded vinyl, somehow carries still
the impress of its owner: trouser-rub

darkening the seat, impatient rhythmic drub
of nails and cigarette on wooden arm,
and round about it shadows of a room,
frayed carpet-corner, mantelpiece, cream walls,
tick of a daily-wind-up clock that fills
resentful silence. No one takes this pew,
because they've never been invited to.

From my father, or of him, I rescued almost random things: objects of no monetary or aesthetic value but imbued with qualities he seemed to represent. I kept his small, hard blue suitcase for important things on holidays; a book-end of a Scottie dog carved by a German prisoner-of-war he befriended; and the pedometer he would race over maps to track the mileage of his swift, loping strides. I wanted his pharmacology notebooks in which, as a student, he had made exquisite drawings of plants and roots with lists of their virtues. But he had long since thrown them out, impatiently, unsentimentally, replacing a side of himself I barely knew with one I knew too well.

From my mother—of her—I gathered several small reminders. One was a two-inch stub of pencil, sharpened with a razor blade and slightly bitten at the end, which she carried in her only handbag to note down prices and times. Her frugality, readiness for emergencies, and a certain anxiousness were still contained in it. Another memento was her Eversharp steel-plated propelling pencil, marked "L Body" on the shaft, with its box of delicate leads. This spoke of her precision, her efficiency (that "L," rather than "Lorna"), as well as her insistence on what was hers. To have her company on walks, I could simply slip it into my pocket: and there she was, setting her chin, stepping out fast, and always quicker than I was to spot the rare flower, the mushroom field, or the weasel that crossed the lane one evening like a small, swift, corrugated shadow.

I took other things. Paper packets of needles and wooden reels of cotton came from the big box whose lid would creak open to the smell of a full draper's shop; each evening she would sit darning or sewing, her hands never idle, even when her fingers grew crooked in old age. The little rotary egg-whisk, with a chipped blue-and-white handle, was one she had used as a child, struggling to beat up whites as forlornly as I did; it said, "Perseverance." At the bottom of a drawer I found a tiny cellophane envelope containing lavender, rose petals, and verbena, priced by her at "25p." (full stop, as always, definitely included). It had long since lost its power to perfume linen, but somehow still breathed thoughtfulness.

Her jewellery was a bag of various plastic beads; her makeup was a single jar of Pond's face cream, used sparingly. I kept her signet ring, although, like her wedding ring, it was worn away almost to nothing, like one you would use to track a bird.

Yet the detail that most neatly caught her was one I could not carry away. It was her crisp in-and-out of breath, an audible wince, as if she was blowing out an infuriating match. She did it when shocked, but also when delighted; when cut by paper, or taking too-hot trays from the oven, but also when preparing to eat chocolate, slowly peeling the silver foil away, or braving a chilly sea, tucking her black curls happily under her plastic cap. That combination of joy, wariness, and briskness made up my mother's life.

She always said she couldn't sing. If I stood beside her in church she would be mostly silent. Occasionally, though, she would clear her throat officially as if about to join in; and with the quick breath she had taken, through almost closed lips, just a little behind the beat, she would hum a note. That uncatchable thing, that sigh in the air, was also her.

2. Seizing

AS I WRITE, A TINY FLY, SMALLER THAN AN ANT, skitters softly from the fruit bowl. Dozens of them flicker in the air today, drawn possibly by the ox-eye daisies fading in their vase, or by the vile-smelling pellets I have put on the bougainvillea. The fly darts one way, then another, skimming the table surface, urgent, driven. I snuff it out. It is so small that it leaves no mark, either on the table or on me. But I feel a pang that is sharp. There was life in that hectic speck: a life that was also mine, in which I was included. Suddenly a mere pulse-in-the-air affects me like a nerve.

It has happened before, just for a second.

> Poised on barbed wire
> the vague crane-fly
> negotiates a steel
> abstraction of itself

> Delicacy alighting,
> a damsel fly

25

> brushes the crude-split
> chestnut fence;
> lays sapphire gauze
> upon the hurt

Tiny,
with golden back
and sand-grain
emerald head,
lifting
its air-light limbs
of fuse-wire
or gold thread,
a beetle drops—
pricks life
across the words I've read

The actions of my own nerves, to spot the beetle, read the words, shake out the book, are instant and hundredfold. How the messages are sent, and in what order, I do not know. Nor do far keener minds. In moments of relaxation, or as he enjoyed some complex question, Jonathan Miller, the opera and film director, liked to rock his long frame back and clasp his hands behind his head. It seemed a fitting gesture of satisfaction with his success. But wearing his neurologist's hat—because he had really meant to be a doctor—he continually asked himself why, and how, he was doing this. First, why was he practising this ridiculously easy thing called art, which he could do with one hand tied behind his back? Was it just weak-mindedness, like that tendency in boyhood always to say yes whenever anyone asked him to play? Was it just an involuntary reaction, like blushing or sneezing? At all events, he could never identify a conscious intention to go into the entertainment line. Accidents of this sort had lured him into *Beyond the Fringe*, the satirical review that first brought him fame—then into directing and, come to that, into long-lasting love—and he wondered how much his own will determined any aspect of his life.

But the problem was much more basic than that. He also wondered, as he leaned back, how the impulse in his brain, to cradle his head in his hands, translated itself to his arms. Was it conscious or unconscious? Did the thought precede the act, as his reason assumed, or accompany it, or even lag behind it? To paraphrase Wittgenstein, what exactly made the difference between "I lift my arms" and "My arms go up"? If he could plumb that, perhaps he would know what life was.

Many other life-mysteries vex human minds. One is the sixth sense, which again seems to waver strangely between action and thought. We come to a door that we have passed many times before and decide, this time, to open it. We do not know why. We enter a room, and instantly something sets up a prickling in the hair, a chill in the veins, and we go no further. It is nothing precisely seen, heard, or felt; it is as if things seen, though mute, also called out, as if things heard also flashed before our eyes, or as if the sense of touch turned its soft fibres inwards, creeping among our thoughts. For some necessary moment we become instinctive, like an animal or a bird.

This odd sense makes us pause, pulling us back from the curb and the unseen car, or pushes us out of danger when the rock falls or the ladder gives way. It says: don't do this.

Yet it is also gentle, like a tap on the shoulder that makes us turn round in the street—to see a tree white and alight with cherry blossom—or look up suddenly from a book, to see four small sunset clouds arranged perfectly over the sea.

Within us or without: Who can tell? That sudden intervention may be subtle as a feather or strong as a pair of arms. In either case, there seems to be a message in it. We look up—why? We are snatched from death—for what purpose? When the blackbird sings in T. S. Eliot's "Burnt Norton," in response to "unheard music hidden in the shrubbery," it alerts the poet to the nature of time: to the voices of children among the rose leaves and the echoes of ghosts, past, present, and future, fused in one moment and one place. "Go, go, go, said the bird: human kind / Cannot bear very much reality." Perhaps only fleeting apprehensions can reveal the reality of life.

Figurative artists know this well. They are obsessed with the life-chase and how fast it escapes, quicker than the ink or paint dries, quicker often than words form. In art schools it is common practice for the first study of an object or a figure to be done in a minute, to catch not the shape or the mass but the life. The material body, with its heaviness and definite outlines, is compression and limitation. Short strokes, almost random, thrown down with speed, seize something more, even if the charcoal snaps and the ink spatters from the pen. That is it.

As a child who grappled with fountain and dip-pens, I felt that ink was live as blood: as prone to stains, spills, and accidents, and as dangerous before it dried, welling and gleaming on the white page. Yet I was also reluctant to use blotting paper, because it crushed something out of what I had drawn, or what I had written.

> I set down words.
> Inside the ink are beads
> that wink and live, like sun
> glistening through rain on glass—
> that will not dry,
> though I puff all my breath
> steadily on them. Fine—
> I'll seize the blotter, press
> their disobedience out. How shy
> my fierceness makes them now,
> fading in their surprise,
> stiffening in helplessness—
> as leaves
> > or birds
> > > or bright fish
> > > > die

The painter Avigdor Arikha felt his compulsion to draw was like a fever, or a telephone ringing; he had to answer at once, work as fast as he could in the here and now, never from memory or notes. It started when he was thirteen, a thin, curly-haired boy in a German labour camp, carrying his sketchbook under his shirt. Quickly, so as not to show what he was doing, he would draw a queue of people waiting for soup, a beggar with his feet wrapped in rags, a naked woman being thrown into a grave. More bodies waited on a cart, like bundles of sticks. He drew on butcher's paper, soft, slightly damp, the sort that absorbs blood. Then the book was thrust inside his shirt again. A camp guard once, noticing him, told him he was playing with fire. Arikha knew he was.

That habit of sketching-as-snatching stayed with him: catching not only human life but the life that quivered in anything. If he drew apples, they were perilously close to the edge of a table. Fresh *baguettes* (he lived later in Paris) still shuddered from being wrenched and torn. In his hallways, doors were opening and shafts of light were disturbed by the passage of bodies. Coats had just been taken off, still warm and swinging, hunched on a hanger with a scarf trailing out of a pocket; umbrellas, just dropped, lay half-open on the floor. He painted his own face shouting, gaping stupidly, glimpsed in a mirror, as if he was determined to take himself by surprise—to throw a stone at himself, he said, and see where it would land. What he could not fail to catch was the "violent hunger" in his eyes. With Samuel Beckett, his best friend, he would sit and talk for hours, every so often leaping up to snare that craggy, thoughtful profile in some transient look: smoking, listening, pushing back his glasses. In Beckett's plays life stood still on the stage, waiting under a tree or trapped to the neck in sand; where it swarmed, surged, chattered endlessly, was in his characters' minds. To pin it down with pastel-stick or brush seemed, to Beckett, impossible. In 1967, wonderingly, he described his friend at work:

> Siege laid again to the impregnable without. Eye and hand
> fevering after the unself. By the hand it unceasingly changes

the eye unceasingly changed. Back and forth the gaze beating against unseeable and unmakeable. Truce for a space.

Arikha knew that in the case of life he was dealing with a trickster, endlessly elusive, constantly flickering, and hinting at a reality that it would not reveal. The Greeks snared some of this in the god Proteus, ever-changing shape from lion, to snake, to water, to a tree. Proteus was assumed to hold the key to the mysteries of Nature, but again he refused to answer questions unless he could be caught.

Alchemists often twinned him with the fleetest life-sparking god, "volatil Hermes," as Milton called him, flashing from Olympus to the sea and darting among the waves "like a seagull catching fish, wetting its whirring wings in tireless brine," in the fifth book of the *Odyssey*. The wide cosmos was his flying ground. His gold-winged sandals gave him that insuperable speed; his gold wand, fluttering with white ribbons, awakened breath or suspended it as he laid it on a man's or woman's eyes. To meddle in human affairs, though, he could take a winsome boyish shape. He invented the shepherd's reed pipe that could carry human music to the gods, and he carried messages from gods to men: a courier as subtle and disguised as the one that tells a man's arm to lift and cradle his head in his hands.

Similar small, clumsy snatches at life fill up my notebooks. Like Arikha, I try to throw them down fast, unrevised, in the moment.

She breezes past,
blonde, pink thighs bare—
he wheels
to compliment
the perfumed air

> Two lovers
> at the bus-stop
> deep-kiss
> once, then twice, again,
> quivering
> with each repeated
> novelty, shivering
> together,
> like the earth in spring

Framed by dark laurels
in his wool-white robe
thought-stilled, a novice stands,
bows his obedient head—
No psalter, but a smartphone
held in his quiet hands.

Like Arikha, I also presume conscious life in anything. Dried seaweed on a beach, gesturing like a tiny black fist towards the unreachable foam; an apple tree astonished by its own dropped fruit; the fruits themselves, red and rot-brown, suddenly jewelled by a gilt wasp; our car headlights, as we pass, petrifying the woods.

SEIZING

Sun strikes the beech:
young ivy twines
delicate emeralds
round her smooth grey neck

Faint-flushed
the moon lies back
in a milk-bath sky

The lowliest bramble
quivers,
jumps,
discerns the rain
before I do

A coin cast
in the beggar's
general direction
glitters like gold
and like contempt

At times life seems all motion, and only motion. Words
must race and tumble out, too, as fast as I can get them down.

Slithering boy down slick rocks
swift in the sea, back-lit,
fragments in ripples, breaks apart
sun-glare in spray-splash,
strives to trap just one bit
in his shivering silk net

When I write the lives of other people, I try to seize movements of this sort: the way they walk, sit in a chair, shrug off a jacket, hold their heads; tiny gestures, snatches of talk. One close friend, when considering something, would put the tips of his fingers to his smiling lips as if in prayer: a reminder that he had once been in the seminary, and now held poetry sacred. Another, a Canadian magistrate, kept the long stare of a man looking out across the prairie, impatient to see to the end of the opposing argument. My father, when sealing a box or folding a tablecloth, would always give it a couple of extra presses, just for luck. My aunt Betty spoke in a high, soft, uncertain voice, as if emerging from a dream of something else.

Some aspects of life, though, are too elusive. When I write at the desk by my Brighton window, a quick shadow often falls. A gull has swooped down from the roof-ridge, but the moment I look up, the bird has gone. It is a quivering of the air, nothing there, timed sometimes to my very act of putting pen to paper. We leap off together. As Eliot wrote in "The Hollow Men":

> Between the idea
> And the reality
> Between the motion
> And the act
> Falls the Shadow

Eliot, I think, meant the shadow of death. But I mean that odd, intruding agency beyond the self, within the self. For me, it is more probably the question that vexed Jonathan

Miller: the precise way in which life and motion are transmitted through the body, and through everything living. To think about it for any length of time is to wrestle with something indefinable, unreachable, taunting ahead, like the green woodpecker in the woods.

> The roused woodpecker flies, and laughs:
> I was never here.
> You saw a branch spring, fields rise up
> green and yellow clear,
>
> but you confused me with the sun's
> sly morning games, or understood
> that leaves fresh out and blown about
> had shown me in the wood—
>
> I called to you from somewhere else,
> not far—not near—
> and though you caught me by my song,
> I was not here!

It took Rumi, the greatest of all Sufi poets, to suggest a different understanding.

> An invisible bird flies over,
> but casts a quick shadow.
>
> What is the body? That shadow of a shadow
> of your love, that somehow contains
> the entire universe.

If poets and painters struggle to catch life, perhaps people with cameras can do better. They can record the instant: the prima ballerina suddenly off-balance, a child jumping from a wall, a soldier falling backwards. That clattering shutter can take ten shots of a hand being lowered to a table. Yet the moment the hand is frozen, life leaves it: no probability before, no possibility afterwards. No wonder some civilisations believe that a photograph extracts the soul.

In a family Victorian wedding photograph a child in arms and a man in a bowler hat in the back row have moved. The baby is completely blurred; the man's face is smudged, like a daub of paint, above a tidy jacket. No one can say now who they were. But then we cannot say who most of the other people are, who have taken pains to dress in their best starched and silk-flower finery and to gather in the garden on what appears to be a broiling day. They sat still for several minutes, serious, none smiling, confident that their lives were being recorded and their identities preserved for evermore. But the babe and the bowler-hatted man knew better and left their fleeting wrigglings instead. They are now the living ones.

How much of life can a camera trap, in any case? Richard Avedon, who photographed America's most famous faces, was not sure. When he snapped Henry Kissinger, then secretary of state and unsparing maker of war on Vietnam and Cambodia, he wanted to show the "anger, ineptitude, strength, vanity, isolation" that seemed, to him, to characterise the man. But the jowly, wary face revealed nothing. The mouth was set. The eyes looked straight at the camera, with just a slight upward tilt of the glasses to the left the only suggestion that a smile could form. The left hand was thrust in the pocket but was not relaxed. "Be kind to me," Kissinger had told him. He then hardened himself for the shot, defensive, distrustful.

Avedon did not want his portraits to have such formality. Nor did he want his subjects artificially smiling, like the picture of his father that used to sit on the family piano—"Smilin' Jack" as they called him, a man he seemed never to have known. He shot in black and white against a white backdrop, the austerity a deliberate foil, he hoped, to the variety and untidiness of life. In this unsparing light he caught Dwight Eisenhower with the look of a surprised baby, Ronald Reagan with a cast of resolution turning into doubt, Marilyn Monroe in a sad dream, Ezra Pound with his thumb in his eye. Like Arikha, he constantly snapped himself off guard, distracted, glaring, hidden by a mask. Yet, as he said again and again, this was not the truth. It was a surface, and that was all he had to work with. Looking at the Kissinger portrait, he asked himself who, or what, it was. Was it just a shadow representation of a man? Or was it closer to a doppelgänger, a likeness with its own life, which might come to replace the original? What really inhabited this face, this body? Whatever it was, he had not caught it; he had simply produced an alternative.

His first piece of fashion photography, for *Harper's Bazaar* in 1946, took models away from their studio poses and put them on a beach, running and jumping with no gloves, no shoes, any old how. In later life in his studio he preserved that practice, showing beautiful women in sulks, unkempt, even frightening. They would never be unaware of the camera, since their job was to court it. But if a curl fell, or a fly buzzed, they could still be snatched off-guard. That remained his ideal.

It was also the technique of the photographer Wang Fuchun, whose work rarely featured in fashionable magazines. His canvas was not the severe white backdrop of a studio but the humid, rickety, teeming "green trains" of China; and his subjects were not the famous but the ordinary. He wanted to catch them as they were, in the instant, before the shock of the wide-open gaze receded and the mask fell. On board the trains, which he rode continually, he would creep about with his camera under his coat and an expression of humble curiosity. He was a strange-looking man, tall and thin, with a long womanish haircut that attracted glances, but a habit of ducking his head to avoid them. He would barely move to take the shot, cupping his hands to his belly as a man might who had eaten well, hoping not to reveal himself or his intentions. Here was a bundled baby popping from a basket, astonishing its mother; a migrant worker, glossy with summer heat and sweat, wriggling along a seat; an elegant woman smoking in a corridor, turning with haughtiness to notice him. As soon as registered, the shot was taken; the shadow of the shutter fell as fast as thought. When he had hesitated—as with his picture of a little peasant girl, face smeared with mud, asleep standing up against a door—he judged his work a failure. It was as if, though asleep, she had struck a pose for him, and he had encouraged her stillness.

How quickly, Wang lamented, people did that, and life stiffened. Migrants camping in the corridor, in a clutter of carpets and pots and pans, clustered into a portrait for him. Tibetan monks made a ritual of offering him a prayer shawl. Lovers canoodling under a blanket, among the emptied supper trays, kept hiding from him and popping out again, giggling, too aware. He took them anyway, snatched love. In the 2000s people seemed to grow even more guarded, resenting his intrusions and reporting him to the authorities. Some of his best work was done when people were completely distracted, half-lost in the crowd: waving their tea-flasks from the train windows for refills at stations, kibitzing around a game of mahjong or, on one of the sleek, modern high-speed trains he never learned to like, shrouding themselves from head to toe in sheets against the icy air-conditioning.

Something about land travel—in buses, coaches, trains— suited his snatching process. As Wang said, people were dislocated there, taken out of time and their familiar place and instead united by heat, thirst, boredom, and the relentless clack of the wheels. Passengers on the trains he haunted, many of them migrating from the countryside for good, created little islands of singularity, with their habits and affections exposed. They lay on straw mattresses or knelt on prayer mats; they opened capacious food tins; played instruments; rigged up ingenious rope cradles; huddled in their padded country jackets to hear a canary in a cage. Some were courteous, deferential; some shoved and spat. He took one photograph, probably staged this time, of a dozen men craning from windows as the train rounded an immense curve in the mountains. Each was reacting differently: grinning, reflective, diffident, worried. Each man was in his own unbounded thought-world as well as the shared life of the train.

As there, so here, on my Monday morning commute from Brighton.

> Nose sharp in his primer
> as a searching pin,
> he learns How to do Business
> With no Risk to him;
> brown Oxfords twitching
> in his ecstasy,
> the 8:15 to London
> flamed with possibility.

> She is old, and as she strokes
> concealer round her eyes
> her mouth sags open unaccountably,
> not to be helped—Across the aisle
> a young man, effortlessly beautiful,
> watches with fascination
> that she should even try

I scribble with my notebook hidden in my lap and, like Wang, I observe. Almost everyone is tapping and coffee-drinking, intent on both. The woman by the far window has taken out her giant peacock-feather earrings, the ones I admired as she came on, and is admiring them herself, though her lobes look sore. The girl beside her, fake-fur collar turned up around her ears, is scrolling fast and anxiously through the weekend emails she ignored. Ahead of me a chiselled young man takes off his enviable loden coat and hangs it on a window hook for all to see. His gesture is calculated, elegant; he knows we are watching. At the table he jerks his laptop open and cracks his fingers like a pianist, knowing we are still looking. The balance of interest in the carriage has now turned to him.

Behind me is a fraught phone conversation about medicine, school, and pickup times. The car that's mentioned, I immediately imagine, is an SUV. The sick child is around eleven, with a ponytail and red-flushed cheeks. The kitchen is bespoke, expensive, with grey stone counters, but today it is a turmoil of bags and books. I know, having leapt there and opened it, that the bathroom cabinet contains a thermometer and a bottle of thick astringent pink stuff. (But they have tried that, and it hasn't worked.) Detail by detail, the life around me invades me. It spills out down suburban streets, crosses seas, revisits the past, plans the future; and all while we are loitering somewhere near Gatwick, where deer stray out of the frosted woods and add, to our running thoughts, their delicate hesitation.

A fascinating interplay also goes on between lives within and outside the carriage: the lives glimpsed for a moment, seized and left behind, like these in Cwmbran, in South Wales.

> Two boys go down the road
> between the railway
> and the business park
> jiggling and half-jostling,
> one bragging, the other

lagging a little, quiet.
They pass into the rain, the mist, the past,
as we aboard the train do; we
whom neither turns to see.

We meet those lives, yet do not enter them. We presume
we must be presences in them, as they are to us—though we
appear as merely a shadow on a street (the shadow passing,
the street remaining) or, at night, a procession of lit carriages
across the sleeping land.

Beyond the window no lights shine.
The sea lies there. We might seek out
its crushing arms, breathe its cold words,
lean to its deeps, but all we see
is our lit capsule and ourselves
messaging contacts to infinity—

Beyond the carriage no lights gleam.
Quiet fields fold out. We might walk there,
feeling for footpaths, guided by
glimmer of glass reed, spectre-spare
sentinel heron; but we see
only ourselves, blank-faced inside the air.

Bede's famous metaphor for human life was a sparrow fly-
ing through a mead-hall on a winter's day, in at one door and
out at another, through the firelit warmth between storms.
His sparrow, too, was a shadow, and it did not linger. It could
have rested and roosted among the thatch and roof beams,

but it recognised no home there. Its life was larger than that. The journey might encompass foul weather, darkness, confusion, but potentially, too, other mead-halls smelling of tallow and beer—or of beeswax, incense, lilies. Centuries before Walt Whitman contained multitudes, a bedraggled Saxon bird suggested both the brevity and the endlessness of life. As we pass through each scene, we absorb something of it, expand to experience it, adventure on.

Since childhood I have played a game I call "Here and there." It is best played from trains. I pick out one object in a landscape—a house, a tree, a far gate—and leap mentally to it, to look back at myself. For a moment, I change places. I cannot make it last any longer, because I sense that if I did so, it would cease to be true; but in that first irresistible second of looking back I am sure it is perfect in every detail, and I feel a thrill as keen as when I capture some stray effect in a word, and note it down.

Inevitably, I am usually too slow. As when a gull flies past my window, I sense the after-beat of life just missed. That gap fills up at once with imaginings. A fire glimpsed in a gully near Crawley, too early in the day, must be secret papers burning. A trio of spindly silver birches, clustered in a flooded field, were perhaps tall sisters just before I saw them, abandoned on some mythical shore. A football on the line at Wandsworth Common is a tragedy for the schoolboys who must have crowded to spot it, still moving slightly, helpless on the track.

> That random arc
> so endless towards the fence

where the ball can't save itself
and won't
return

And sudden flowers, like the swooping gull, are seen
too late.

A flash of primroses
bright-banked
beneath brown woods
distracts him
from his screen
too late
to work out
why

Gazing from the window, I extrapolate life across the
landscape. I imagine the lithe young man who has sprayed
"10 Foot" in enormous left-leaning letters on sooty walls from
Brighton to London Bridge, slithering down in jeans, shelter-
ing in that niche from the thundering trains, pressing his back
against the bricks. The can is in his hand, still primed. I see
the viticulturist who has expertly laid out a little triangular
vineyard in a Croydon allotment: an Italian probably, run-
ning a restaurant perhaps, bending and twisting the vines. In
my mind he wears a blue apron, and his neighbours (who may
get a bottle of the vintage) rest on their spades, marvelling.
An old listing caravan in a copse near Three Bridges, once
white, now lightly mouldered over, speaks of illicit smokes

and sex. A car in a deep lane fascinates me, crawling between two points I do not know; I wonder if even the driver is sure where this road goes, between the high hedges crowding on either side. For a second I feel some connection, a shiver of sympathetic contact. Then we've moved on. I shall never answer those questions, I leave them behind—as I also left that patient horse, blinkered in a field of mud somewhere in Gloucestershire, covered in a grey blanket, waiting.

On Inner London bus journeys, moving far more slowly, I do not need imaginings. From the upper deck, my notebook hidden by my bag, my sleeve regularly wiping away accumulated breath, I pick up lives. One March morning a woman comes to the side door of Quinn's lounge in Kentish Town ("Black Bush Irish Stout," shouts the wall) and shakes out a mat. Her action belies the impression, from the peeling blue-and-yellow paint, that the place is closing down. On the other hand, she is in slippers, the room behind is dark, and she doesn't scan the street for punters as publicans do. Her shaking of the mat may be efficient, or angry; it is hard to tell. I puzzle over her, wondering whether she is Irish or, from her fine cheekbones, Polish. Or neither.

A corner intervenes, the scene shifts. A young Black man in dreadlocks and hi-viz, carrying a guitar, strolls through the neglected little park under the railway bridge. That spot is worth a poem in itself, where life usually lurks in a hoodie, sulking, smoking.

The tiny park
that no one sees,
new-rinsed, willow-springing
in a sweet breeze
forgets its usual
liveries,
blue-and-white crime-tape
between the trees.

His trainers are new, blindingly white; his step is loose.
He is probably going to busk by the station, but to me he
represents spring, a harbinger-angel. Further on, the Turkish
man who runs the hardware shop counts out money in a cor-
ner, finds it exact, clenches it, stares over the top of his glasses
at the receipt spooling out of the till; business is picking up,
and those gleaming buckets and brushes may be gone by the
end of the day. A builder struggles to cross the road under a
piece of chipboard, rests on the pavement with it; he is too
fat, winded, should give up the cigarettes that bulge in his
breast pocket, as his doctor has already warned him. As the
bus passes, he blows out his cheeks again.

These lives are part of mine now, and they go curiously
deep. I never felt this so keenly as when I travelled through
India, cocooned in a white Ambassador car whose driver
rested his arm almost permanently on the horn. Along the
road came lordly wagons, covered with dust and hand-painted
warnings ("Horn Please," "Use Dipper at Night"); swaying
camels, dangerously unlit at night, pulling carts among the
potholes; tractors festooned with holy tinsel; and buses with
last-minute passengers clinging on behind. Squadrons of

workers in shining bleached shirts rode by on high Hercules bikes, straight-backed and proud, with a purpose. Bicycle-rickshaws wove through the traffic with improbably large loads of maize stalks, Calor-gas cylinders or blue plastic piping; walkers carried huge piles of dishcloths and dusters, or yellow-flowering branches from the Pride of India tree. One man staggered under a sack of cement, another under a filing cabinet as big as himself in which yet more lives, in the form of invoices, permissions, orders, and certificates, could be appropriately stored. All around the vast organism of India hummed, blared, and thronged, but without a hint of chaos, as though the common enterprise of living united everyone.

In these fleeting observations I sometimes catch, as in a mirror, eyes looking directly back. For a moment, disconcertingly, separate lives flow together, as when I saw two small boys stalking a fox in the Kemp Town Enclosures, in a summer twilight.

> At dusk
> the fox,
> a brownish blur,
> slinks from the coverts.
> The boys are waiting.
>
> Still, on all fours,
> heads down,

knuckles rubbing
the dry ground.

Grey leaves,
dark underspace,
lean twist and tang,
the fox.

The boys.

Soft-padded, silent,
watching each
the other
that is not quite
the other:
lines of definition
and of separation
tentatively
misting

To become the other is unsettling, a widening of being
that moves the heart until it fades to strange; until, like Wang
Fuchun with his camera, I regret the trespass, or fear it, and
look away.

Startlingly close
to the window
of the bus
she's still in bed,
sitting up

in black lace singlet,
summer duvet
chastely spread—
She's adjusting
glitter-bangles
on her arms.
I turn my head.

Framed in a casement,
her soft red hair
carefully parted,
perfect as Vermeer
her face pale oval
ivory serene,
lit from below
by the ravening screen

That girl, in a Gower Street office, looked up and saw
me. She raised her hand, disordering her hair, consciously
or unconsciously, however that is done. A single beat passed
until the wide-open gaze receded and the mask fell. The next
moment, what? Her eye was distracted by some new mes-
sage; a colleague brought in coffee. Our lives moved apart,
unsynchronised, and we no longer understood each other.
A similar melding can happen when rescuing lives from the
past. After long immersion, rightly or wrongly, biographers
sense how their subject will eat, enter a room, put on a cloak,
contemplate a battle. I felt I knew how Pilate would react
to the tedious, uncomfortable process of being shaved by a
slave, without soap; how "Perkin Warbeck" would feel when

being tight-laced into armour for jousting, at which he was no good; how bitter wild plums and barley bread would taste in the mouth of Orpheus, another of my subjects, whose heavenly voice was toned with milk and honey.

With these sensory connections, moods came too. Writing about Pilate brought spells of black frustration and irritation with the world in general, as if I, too, was trapped, like him, out of my depth in a job without prestige. Entering the life of Shelley was permanently exhausting, exhilarating, fraught; I would find myself at dinner parties suddenly holding forth on the freedom of the press or the rights of man, shocking myself as much as anyone else. Because, for a while, I was more than myself.

Richard Avedon reported much the same thing. He had to take pictures, as I have to write, in order to feel truly alive. Yet taking them was also a way of discovering who he was. Each new subject—William Casby, born in slavery, with his desperate face like worn, hewn wood; Boyd Fortin, a thirteen-year-old rattlesnake butcher, holding the draped skin against his bloodied apron; Ronald Fischer, beekeeper, letting his charges swarm across his bald, impassive body— brought out in him aspects of himself. Even Henry Kissinger reflected some part of him. Avedon's autobiography consisted of three hundred portraits of other people.

"We have all of us one human heart," Wordsworth wrote. That thought convinced him that his poetry would last. Bob Marley sang the same. "One Love! One Heart! Let's get together and feel all right." One heart; one common air; and, perhaps, one life, present, future, past.

3. Indwelling

SNOW BELONGS TO THE PAST. ALMOST ALL MY MEMO-
ries of deep snow, the sort that obliterates and then remakes
the world, contain the faint faces of grandparents and long-
vanished aunts. They stare from the busy fire through the
window where snow is falling, ephemeral in that window
as the flakes that melt against the glass. In another scene I
am in a suburban lane, just past the railway bridge, and as
the gritty specks begin to whiten the hedges a vague hand
takes mine, less solid than the landscape, and tucks it in
the pocket of an outmoded coat. Somewhere in mid-Kent
a train on which my family seem to be the only passengers
slides to a halt between great buttresses of snow. A guard
jumps out to clear the track, wielding a cricket bat instead
of a spade.

So much for memories. One recent February, more scien-
tifically, I tried to monitor a north London fall. On the 2nd
it began, dropping big, floppy flakes that melted before they
settled. But it did not stop. Out among the redbrick terraces,

quiet deepened and accumulated. By the 3rd the flakes were small, hard, and determined, and the sky iron-grey. In a few hours, I told myself eagerly, Parliament Hill would be smoothly covered.

The ancient Thracians, Herodotus reported, thought of snow as feathers shaken out of the sky. There is an impression of caressing, almost of warmth, in that. The word that best suits walking in snow is *footfall* rather than *footstep*; for where a footstep announces and proceeds, a footfall vanishes. It is softer, muffled, sinking further into the white; stealthy, surreptitious, and hopeful, like a thief in the night. It becomes part of the general conjuring act of the snow, where furrows, paths, and roads disappear, hedges are drifted over, near slopes and distant Downs are made one unmarked page, and all the distinctions and divisions humans make—their efforts of digging, ploughing, marking, and dividing to show what is theirs and what another's—are buried deep. For a while even Camden Council's parking signs are dusted into oblivion, and everything is permitted.

Yet I had learned from the conductor Claudio Abbado, when I wrote of him, that there was a certain sound to snow. If you stood on a balcony, he said, you might become aware of it. It was a falling, fading away to nothing, *pianissimo*, like breath itself. You could hear it only if you listened to what some supposed was silence.

He had also added to the sound of the snow. When he wished to reflect on the scores that were perfectly memorised in his head he would walk in the Alps near the Matterhorn, letting the music dwell and linger among the towering peaks. It was inaudible, doubtless, to anyone but him. But by that glacier, or on that crag where a lone pine leaned before the wind, some phrase or section would be left behind in memory. He might also hear, as he walked, the map of music he had created there before.

Around it, silence reigned. It was the silence he knew already, between the moment when he raised his baton and when it fell. That same alert, rapt trembling followed his performances of Mozart's Requiem, for a whole minute after that final *"quia pius es,"* or Bruckner's Ninth, for three minutes after the last note had died away: the vanishing of music, that magic life-form, always to be recreated, never in the same way twice. It was the stilled breath of an audience too transfixed to applaud but, at any moment, bound to rise and shout. A stillness that contained both echoes past and the expectation of life.

By late afternoon on the second day, the snow had done its work. Parked cars stood blinded in the street, and the drains and bins were dredged with white. Everything was smothered, astonished, as if asking what to do next. What I did was to pull on my boots, because I was going out to record life as it emerged from oblivion again.

Sounds recorded (black notebook):
Muffled footsteps / footfalls, mine.
Carrion crows cawing: nearby, rude and harsh; far away, faint and plaintive.
Woman's call: "Rufus, come OUT of there!"
Bells of All Hallows (Big Ben effect): five o'clock.
Shouts and yells of youths ambushed by snowballs: "I told my mum I'd be home by now!"

More footsteps. Powder snow rustles; ice makes a crisp snap;
icy footholds in dry snow creak under the boots.

5:09 train to Richmond (still running!). Robin singing some-
where.

Police siren, Mansfield Road. Two clacking parakeets overhead.

Child, crying: "You SAID we could go on the big hill."

Bells of All Hallows: quarter-past.

The snow had not silenced Parliament Hill for long. But
into the muted air, there and beyond, human pitch and tone
wove perfectly. As the misted sun sank down, glowing pink
across the snow, no man-made noise seemed out of place.
Once more, we had colonised the cold white strangeness with
our breathing and our ghosts.

I, too, was reclaiming the hill, scribbling it back into
my own life. With snow, it has no history. Without snow, it
is covered with memory-markers, thickets of them in some
places. (There is the spot where the boys began a stick fight
as I described the beauty of a beech tree; there the corner
where the dog, lost for an afternoon, came nonchalantly trot-
ting out; there the pond bank where we waited one freezing
morning, binoculars ready, for the bittern that never was.)
Both the hill and Hampstead Heath beside it are loud, too,
with poems I've attempted, still clinging to paths and trees.
Above the football pitch, dead leaves will always dance past
in fantastic formations, as I saw them once; on the Highgate
slope a small apple tree, bent across a boggy patch, will
always be mistaken for a rose; and a weeping willow by the
men's bathing pond will always contain the bird I heard

there, pure green water-notes dripping through the leaves. On a woodside bench in the summer someone left a copy of Trollope's *Barchester Towers*, and I read it until the light faded; until I wrote a poem of the sun leaving and dusk, like a slow blind, sliding in.

> He has said goodbye,
> he who gave heft
> and a hearty laugh
> to girlish conversation—
> now, as night spreads
> on the whispering lawn,
> timidly drawn together,
> they talk of him.

My working week is usually divided between two cities, Brighton and London. In both I am close to open country—in London, admittedly, just the small, miraculous patch that is Hampstead Heath—and out there, wandering as I do, I often walk with ghosts. The cities themselves rarely summon them, too distracting, too built-over and thronging with contemporary folk; though there are alleyways in central London, and neglected wooden jetties by the Thames shore, where I have smelt ghosts or half-met them, unloading furs from Muscovy or scarpering after picking a quick pocket.

On the hills, by contrast, past lives seem intrinsic as

stone. Tool-workings, quarries, tumuli, and terraces mark them all over, unobscured by the plantings of the present day. (Even Parliament Hill has its tumulus, railed off and crowned with dark Victorian trees. Sometimes, sheep are even grazed there.) If I sit in the lee of a burial mound, out of the bitter wind, shades of Neolithic hunters creep through the grass. Their broad, ugly, kindly faces watch in the sunlight as I write, and their breathing is quiet under the ridge.

In spring pale-pink restharrow creeps across the Downs. The name itself brings out ghosts, this time medieval ones: the peasant casting aside his wooden plough and flopping down himself, sweating on a spring day as the earth breaks up in flints; the labourer swigging from the leather flask at his waist, or huddling under a hedge from sudden rain. Village folk, especially when working together to reap or glean, used to sing in these fields, easing the monotony of the task as sailors with their shanties eased the rigours of the sea. Tremors of those old songs still seem to blow through. The very rise and dip of paths calls up the long-distance journeyman, bent under a pack of tools, or the pilgrim with scrip, staff, and woollen hood heavy with lead badges. Back on Hampstead Heath again I can stray into the ancient forest of Middlesex, a royal hunting ground, where gold and velvet may flash through the great trees, with a whirl of cloaks and a drumming of close-packed hooves. Below the work-and-therapy chat of modern joggers floats the faint tantivy of horns. They have passed here, and they are hardly any distance ahead—if I run, I will catch them up, before the woods close round them.

Sometimes the ghosts are ancient painted figures. From
the walls of Clayton church, under Ditchling Beacon, they
climb stiffly down, Byzantine deacons and disciples emerg-
ing from dim whitewash to take colour in the air.

At dusk they start to stir, the painted dancers,
fade from the plastered walls,
belt up their long slim robes, and clear the wood
before the screech-owl calls,

to crest the hill and take their place, wind-shivered,
bending each close-cropped head
forward to some faint music, each gaunt limb
to one another's tread,

swaying and turning in their rounds, these dancers,
weaving so late, so long,
that white tracks have been worn to valleys, ridged
with harebell banks of song.

The running fox, frost-furred, has watched them circling
with his swift starveling stare—
their hands held ritually, straight-fingered
in terror or in prayer—

and then he sees them vanishing, these dancers,
running from rough turf rings
down to the church, the walls, rigidity.
Under the dawn-touched hill a blackbird sings.

I met another ancient ghost in the tiny church at Patricio in rainy mid-Wales: a church backed into a rocky slope and approached past a dark, sunken stream. In a room at the west end its founder-saint, Issui, watched me with his one good eye. The tiny window beside him was filled with the bracken-brown flank of the mountain.

He owns this church,
carries it
like a swung purse at his belt.

One wall-eye,
one ragged robe,
all else he has.

His bird-thin bones
are nestled here,
blessed six times over.

Black dripping woods,
pink rosebay stems
surround his well;

if you climb down there,
throw a coin.
Remember him.

Through his squint window
he holds close
the mountain sleeping.

Some of my ghosts, though, are modern. In summer, out
of term, the voices of twenty-first-century boys rise from the
scoop of field in the clifftop that is the cricket pitch for Bede's
school in Eastbourne, perilously overhanging the sea.

The sacred square is level, more or less.
The board, a little sideways, clearly reads
"Last inns," and "Wickets 9" and "Overs 6."

Daisies have colonised its loneliness,
the bumpy outfield lost in bramble-weeds
and hanging elder, where a loud bird clicks

and flies, like some irked umpire from the press
of "Howzat?!" as the anguished bowler pleads
while rueful batsman prods the standing sticks—

No other sound disturbs the emptiness.
Blue sky meets sea, and one thin pathway leads
into the wood, where summer preens and flicks,
dreaming of wickets nine and overs six.

The deep-worn path from Woodingdean to Lewes, called
Juggs Lane, has the noisiest ghosts. There I follow nineteenth-
century fishwives, in pattens and tucked-up skirts, carrying
herring and mackerel from Brighton to the towns inland.
They tell vulgar tales and show their crooked, gappy teeth
like horses when they laugh. If it rains, their shoes slip
on the chalk, as mine do, and I take their recommenda-
tion to walk where the gravelly stones have been washed

down, carving out the track as they have done. When I pick blackberries on the path under Kingston Ridge they raid the bushes with me, their tanned, sinewy arms oblivious to scratches, their mouths purple with juice. They walk the seven miles, and walk them back, with no option of catching the bus at one end of the journey; just a pause for a drink of beer, a readjustment of hairpins and a hitch of fishy stockings, the baskets now light on their shoulders, before they must return again.

Other crowds jostle in this landscape. The present-day walkers and bikers I meet add their own worlds, their preoccupations, the cramps, or skids that happened here or over there, the people greeted and those being inwardly brooded over, each as vivid as the other. On Beddingham Hill the view north from the radio masts will always be as it appeared to the artist I met one August, ponytailed, straw-hatted, with ribbons in his grey beard and a sweat-soaked shirt open to the waist. He had ridden his bike-and-cart over from Newhaven to sell bags of kindling and buy canvases. As we talked, the valley below became a wide Field of Folk filled with kindling-buyers (especially at the Trevor Arms in Glynde, now closed down), canvas-sellers in Lewes, customers from the post office where he used to work before they brought in vans. For him, that part of the hill was where he had picked up a 1945 penny, almost unscratched, therefore dropped not long ago, and where his wife had found three pounds scattered around, so that now they were always on the lookout. He thought he might find Iron Age coins if he was lucky, past and future joyfully colliding in his head. As he set off again he said he would be looking for snails, moving them to the side of the path if they seemed in danger, and that I should do the same, because all life was sacred. We shook hands on that, and his parallel universe bumped away.

Beddingham Hill records only a village. Other local hills and valleys have names—Hard Dole, Breaky Bottom, Starvel Ridge—that ensoul them both with the striving, shivering poor and with characters of their own. Sometimes the names commemorate a momentary thing: a scare, a cold crouch against the wind, or a track lost among impenetrable gorse for which the rough land is to blame. One slope of footpath near Mile Oak, much like any other, is called Rest and Be Thankful, where some weary walker has endowed the long hill with a Sarsen stone and kindness.

Some places I have named myself. The northern side of Cattle Hill in Ovingdean is now Goshawk Ridge, after I saw two men leap from a van, well gloved, and scramble to release one. The flailing brown flash of the great bird became an indelible part of the hill. The path below I called Adonis Corner after the butterfly that suddenly kindled at the field-edge, a flame of a blue for which I did not (and do not) have the words. The grass there has trembled ever since with the breath-quick possibility of beauty. Elsewhere, I keep in mind the prompts of long-gone people. Passing below Bird Brow, a tiny high valley with sides so steep that the cows teeter like cutouts, I watch for starlings or pigeons to spring from the crest. At poverty-stricken Whitehawk in East Brighton, on a path with the racecourse grandstand on one side and, on the other, a tide of scrubby bushes jumbled with car seats and plastic bags, I still anticipate a shining bird hovering and plunging out of the sky.

Margaret Gelling would have seen that bird. She worked for the English Place-Name Society from 1946, studying the origin of place-names and thus the hidden life of the land. She was a neat, keen, merry woman—"prissy" as she described herself, sensibly shod and clad. The gear was appropriate for slopping through *slaep, fenn, myrr,* and *slohtre* (the disappointing origin of Upper and Lower Slaughter) or stomping through *leah, hurst, holt,* and *graefe,* where trees were felled and coppiced and axes rang in the woods.

She spent much of the time with her nose in one-inch Ordnance Survey maps: a coarse instrument for her purpose, but nonetheless teeming with life as soon as she briskly shook them out. There ran the roads, past dense blots of woods and gritty amalgams of towns; past orchards that someone had carefully planted, canals that a Dutchman had probably cut, a stately home positioned with a view pleasing to the architects in their tall black hats, and a tunnel driven straight and true by Irish railway navvies through the rock. At the sign for an inn, carriages slowed and ostlers bustled out; while beside the Gothic typeface that marked an abbey men and women entered quietly to the gathered breath of incense and knelt down.

Her work appealed deeply to her socialist, even communist, instincts. Most of the place-names of England had been bestowed not by officialdom, or in deference to knights, earls, or kings, but by ordinary peasants coping with flooded pasture or looking over the hills. That habit had long died out; people assumed it was all done ages since. But as a resident of Birmingham ("village of Beorma's people"), Margaret liked to think that Spaghetti Junction, the giant intersection where the M6 and A38 intertwine, was a rare modern example of the will of the people expressed in a name. Otherwise, her mission was to summon up the active world the Anglo-Saxons made: to restore to Brewerne in Cambridgeshire its pungent beer smell, and to Colerne in Wiltshire its dusting of charcoal on sacks, spades, and men.

Even more pleasing, though, was to uncover the ancient life under suburbs, stripping away with her derivations the faux-Tudor and mock-Georgian, pebbledash and prefab industrial, to leave a simpler scene. Thus, in the soulless tracts of south London, Penge became "pond's end," a shimmering place, perhaps with willows; Norwood became "the Great North Wood," flickering with shields and dark dragons; and Croydon, now crammed with office towers like a mini Chicago, became "the vale where the wild saffron grows." Stumbling one day out of what remains of the Great North Wood, I came upon a mighty oak, a survivor wedged into a driveway on a suburban street. The tarmac around it was humped and scarred, as if it still fought old battles in the Saxon dirt; clenched fists bulged from its ravaged hide, and its branches seemed pinioned with swords.

For Cedric Robinson, the land's life could be felt under his feet. He was the longest-serving Queen's Guide to the great sands of Morecambe Bay in Lancashire. It was possibly the most dangerous place in England: 311 square kilometres of ever-changing mudflats, sandbanks, channels, and quicksands. He had once seen a fisherman's tractor with all its gear disappear in just two seconds. Horses and carts vanished too. The main rivers of the sands, the Kent and the Leven, could displace themselves invisibly, so that only his sinking ashplant felt them under the mud. In 2004 twenty-three Chinese cockle-pickers, in the pay of a gangmaster, were drowned there as they worked at night, leaving behind strange, short rakes that Cedric had not seen before. They could have had no idea that the tidal range was 10.5 metres, one of the biggest in the world, or that the water could sweep round from all directions—"the meetings," his fisherman father called them—to make escape impossible. The sands changed, he reckoned, about one hundred times a day. Even some of the other fishermen, when there were twenty-four in his village of Flookburgh rather than two, were afraid of the sands and would hang back, rather than go first, when they all set off to walk to the channels.

But ancient travellers found the sands a useful shortcut between Lancaster and Kendal, so they chanced them all the same. Since the sixteenth century more than one hundred had drowned crossing them. Hence the job Cedric Robinson held, which had now morphed into escorting parties of schoolchildren, dogs, outdoorsmen, housewives, and stiff old folk, whom he kept from straying with firm blasts of his whistle. Each time he set a new path for the walkers he took across—about nine miles in all, from Kents Bank to Arnside—he would test it first with the weight of his lean fisherman's body, then with the probe of his ashplant, then sometimes with the weight of his tractor, to see if it was safe. If it was, he marked it out with branches of laurel, thinking each time, *How long will this last?* Long enough, but no more; for the tide came in like a galloping horse. He had adapted to this live landscape by working on it, man and boy, catching flounder in staked-out nets and rocking on a board until the sand started spitting up cockles, as if it was raining; revelling in the cascading starlings, the gorgeous sunsets and the flocks of gulls that rose before the tide. For as long as he was able he shed his shoes, seized his stick, and headed out into a glittering world that was never the same twice—with a flask of milky tea in his haversack and the tide times written on his hand.

Even in more permanent places, the land can glow with life of its own. On days of mist or snow the emptier hills and valleys lie like creatures still breathing, as if sheets have been thrown over sleeping bodies or muslin drawn across a face.

> Dawn mist
> obscures
> but beautifies,
> matt powder
> brushed
> upon a cheek,

while sharp-nibbed frost
defines, conceals
the raw-boned shyness
of the fields—

> As if a god lay there asleep,
> shoulder and arm and hip.

By day my local hills rise up like companions, urging me to walk both on them and with them. They offer gorse-lined hollows against the wind, soft turf paths, and a rolling, inviting motion as seductive as the sea. Like the sea, they also cast up treasure: sapphire milkwort and gold tormentil glowing from the shoals of droppings left by rabbits and sheep. As I walked near Wilmington once, dark shadows in a rubble bank surprised me; I looked closer and they were violets, seemingly generated then and there by the hill itself.

> The chalk
> had violets in it,
> scumbled in shadow,
> blue as flint;
> when I paused,
> one beat,
> they spilled out at my feet

At night the hills brood, their crouching power compacted in darkness. One or two slight clouds, servants and attendants, may haunt the tops in case they stir—as one or two drift always at the flattened, exploded peak of Etna, keeping watch as the volcano sleeps. To walk on these hills is to trespass on a presence.

The boy Wordsworth felt this strongly and recorded his shivers of sympathy and fear in *The Prelude.* Out on the hills at night alone, burdened with springes to catch woodcocks, he would sometimes steal a bird from another boy's trap; and then he would seem to hear, on the empty fells,

> Low breathings coming after me, and sounds
> Of undistinguishable motion, steps
> Almost as silent as the turf they trod.

On another occasion, fear became terror. As he rowed alone at night on a lake in Patterdale, a great cliff

> As if with voluntary power instinct
> Upreared its head. I struck and struck again,
> And growing still in stature the grim shape
> Towered up between me and the stars, and still,
> For so it seemed, with purpose of its own
> And measured motion, like a living thing,
> Strode after me.

Shaking, he rowed his boat back to the shelter of the willow tree where he had found it. For days afterwards he lived with a strange, undetermined awareness of "unknown modes of being." This was troubling at first, giving him bad dreams. But gradually, over years, his fear became a heightened sense of consciousness in everything.

> To every natural form, rock, fruit, or flower
> Even the loose stones that cover the highway
> I gave a moral life; I saw them feel,
> Or linked them to some feeling: the great mass
> Lay bedded in a quickening soul, and all
> That I beheld respired with inward meaning.

He and they composed a "sentiment of Being." And that being spread

> O'er all that moves and all that seemeth still;
> O'er all that, lost beyond the reach of thought

And human knowledge, to the human eye
Invisible, yet liveth to the heart . . .

From trespass then, the poet moved to understanding.

On a wooded hillside in Umbria I, too, committed such a trespass. It was broad daylight, near noon; the wood, of beech, bush-heather, and galled sapling oaks, was dense, hot, and dry. As I paused at the top of a rocky section I heard breathing, the susurration of deep sleep, rhythmic and faintly rasping. It was too loud to be human, and nothing larger lived in this place. It had to be close at hand, in those trees, just over my shoulder, but I could see nothing. Only the slightest wind trembled the leaves, and the softest gulps the inky little stream.

It must be wild boar, I thought. We would hear them at dusk, rustling and rooting in the undergrowth as we sat with our Camparis on the terrace, watching for the first star. But as the breathing went on, continuous as a machine, yet living, I realised that the whole landscape was somehow held in it: not only the trees of the wood, the walkers, the rocks, but the little town of Mercatale in the valley, where the blinds were being lowered for lunch and the *ravioli in brodo* was being ladled out; not only me, but the traffic on the road to Cortona, and shining Lake Trasimeno beyond. As I came back down, the pink cyclamen that glowed from the leaf-litter seemed, like those Sussex violets, to have been breathed to the surface by a god.

An alternative thought was that I was the one breathing. I was the one in whom this landscape was contained, who was arranging it and naming it, only half helped by the dog-eared photocopied map borrowed from our *pensione*. A second eye might read it in a completely different way. Certainly the old man I met, pruning an olive tree with a sickle in a tiny overgrown meadow, would describe and explain the woods with the proper words that belonged to them. Seen by him, a dweller among the trees that dwelt in him, they became a deeper and another place.

Marie Smith did this service for the vast spruce tundra of the Copper River Delta in Alaska. She was the last inhabitant to speak the Eyak language, which died with her: she held the words, and the words composed the land. Only she could address as *c'a* the silky, gummy mud that squished between her toes when she walked by the shore, or call the tangled driftwood *'u'l*, using a different word for it if it was in one piece. For the parts of the spruce, the prevailing tree, she had dozens of words. *Lis* was the neat, conical tree itself, *gahdg* the blue-green needles that carpeted the ground and could be brewed up for tea, *sihx* the creeping sap that was smeared onto caulk canoes. As I wrote these words, which I had no idea how to say, they became an incantation, summoning the spirit of the land until I walked among spruces no longer squat and dull but silvered, precious, tall, breathing out the resinous elixir of Copper River Delta life.

Eyak was also rich in words for the other essentials of this place: for black abalone, red abalone, ribbon-weed and tubular kelp, drag nets and dipping nets and different sizes of rope. One word, *demexch*, was a soft and treacherous spot in the ice over a body of water, where a man, with care, might crouch and fish. Marie Smith, by saying or even thinking the word, called up his shadow hunched in the furs and sealskins of another age. Salmon was a staple here; she made every part of the fish noble by naming it in Eyak, as well as the separate stems and shoots of the salmonberries served with the dried roe. In the cannery where she worked, no one else paid such respectful attention to foraged food anymore. Nor did they know that by using the same word, *kultahl*, for both feathers and the leaves of deciduous trees, she was acknowledging that these things shared the same organic being.

On the other side of the world Dr. Geoffrey Yunupingu, the blind singer whose voice was said to be the most beautiful in Australia, took on the spirit of his totemic animal, Baru the saltwater crocodile, to remake the land. Baru had wandered in the Dreamtime through the landscape of Elcho Island, off northeast Arnhem Land, naming the red cliffs, the mangrove swamps, the creeks, and stringybark trees. On one wide beach the boy's aunts set up various sizes of tin cans in a row and gave him sticks, so that this sightless child could sing the scene for himself in the steps of the ancestors.

When, many years later, he performed in London, China, and New York, and when he won standing ovations at the Sydney Opera House, this was what he was doing. Almost no one knew. The high plaintive tenderness of his voice and his guitar were all that mattered to his audience. Yet to him, sitting almost motionless onstage, a slight figure in a leather jacket and with the inward stare of the blind, his songs of orange-footed scrubfowl evoked the keening of long-dead women scratching the dry earth to live, and his thunderheads over the sea were the forms of ancestral spirits. The name of his backing group, the Saltwater Band, gave a clue to what was happening.

In his last months, needing frequent dialysis, he still occasionally struggled back to Elcho Island, where the ancestors had determined that he should go to die. He made a shallow pit in the sand and slept there sometimes. A few *Balanda*— white folk—thought he was just long-grassing, sleeping rough like other drunks. Instead he was listening to the waves, and to Baru's old creation-songs.

Up on my white cliffs one summer day, near a grassy hollow with a marker for an ancient church, I, too, paused to think of ancestors.

> Out on the naked Down a shallow dip
> shelters a stone. Sea-winds alone and sheep
> are congregation here, where for a space
> the Sanctus rang. I wonder if the priest
> wore vestments proper as these mallow flowers
> that splash their churchly purple in the grass.
> It seems unlikely. But the new-shorn sheep
> creep up, heads bowed, with looks of *pietas*.

Around me the hills stretched out their long, curved limbs; the blue sky hazed above me, as if with winter breath. Gulls floated in it, held aloft by a sound of distant sighing. In the wide cup of the land the sea moved and shifted, a great creature sleeping.

To those who live beside it, the sea dominates everything. My morning ritual is to check on its mood and colour and the texture of the waves. They are never the same twice. The rippling layers of green light and blue shade may give way to a grey dark as pewter or a light beige, like sand. The horizon is ruler-sharp or may disappear entirely, sky and sea combining.

Day after day, making and unmaking are the sea's business. The supposedly fixed forms of the world are continually reinterpreted and re-deciphered. Waves stipple and dapple like the skin of a beast, gather all over like ruched silk or pulsate, barely moving, beneath an untroubled sky. At dusk the whole surface may thicken to velvet, its blue pile delicately shifting towards the night. Southwesterlies outrage the sea, but under northeasterlies it labours to move, furious, tide and wind negating each other. Every cloud is pulled down to float on it, in fragments or in broad spreading shawls.

The sea also carries the histories of all who have sailed on it. It heaves with the rock and wreck of ships, swells with filled nets and spilled oil, reflects the blinking lighthouse, the smuggler's lantern, and the creeping lights of mackerel boats. When its storm-waves smash against promenades and breakwaters, photographers delight to find in the spray the faces of Poseidon or the Furies. The voices it mostly carries, though, are those "that will not be drowned," as Maggi Hambling's giant steel scallop shell proclaims on the beach at Aldeburgh: the unforgotten, the still there. Even on windless nights the sea can roar like a stadium of human shouts, and in calmer moods it flows easily through human words, written or in conversation. There are few better endings for a stanza or a paragraph than "the sea," the natural limit beyond which it seems we cannot go, at which we must pause—until we go on.

Yet despite all this, I also forget the sea. Above the noise of traffic, it can sometimes barely be heard from the promenade. The chorus of dawn birds is often louder. The sea's presence is such a constant that I may go most of a day without observing it, or even registering that it is there. I sit beside it, reading or working, as though this immensity and myself are unremarkable partners. At a nearby beach café wind-blown punters do the same, queuing behind the seawall for the legendary bacon sandwiches and mugs of tea, while on the other side of the wall huge symbols drawn in chalk (who knows by whom?) address the sea as Alpha and Omega, the beginning and the end, the infinite one.

These interweavings of lives are old and deep. The sea is mysteriously connected with me in its chemical composition, its pulses, and its tides. At the dawn of time the first peculiar land creatures flopped out of it and sucked in air, on a beach such as this. Each time I gaze directly at the sea, as a strip in the distance or the blue that fills my windows, it shouts, "I am!" as a god might declare it, boundless in being and power. One March day of flashing, wind-driven brightness, that shout was a trembling in my own blood, as if it said, "We are infinite together."

This was the voice I seemed to hear again, by the site of the ancient church. Not God capitalised, patriarchal, hung about with baggage, but the life-force itself, ineffable and invisible. That presiding, moving presence, in both hills and distant sea, was irresistible. Yet it was also inward, and touchingly familiar: like a friend who suddenly, in the ease of summer, had begun to sing quite softly into my ear. "I am nearer than your jugular vein," murmured Rumi's God to the poet. So near that my breathing, and the breathing scene, became the same.

4. Returning

"DEEP BREATH," SAYS THE DOCTOR. I TAKE ONE, AND hold it. The stethoscope is cold on my chest, colder on my back. The doctor makes a loose fist and goes over my upper torso, knocking. I sound hollow, like dead wood, or like a shell: a reminder that almost all my body, save less than 0.1 percent of it, is empty space.

On every side brisk instruments have been measuring my signs of life. Numbers race up and down on the blood-pressure gauge. The ECG machine has spilled out its graph paper covered with spikes and troughs. A glass tube under my tongue checks I have no fever. My blood has already been tapped and sorted by barcode, my urine categorised by slips of card tipped with chemical reagent. If they admit me, I will be woken every three hours for the thermometer and the blood-pressure clamp to check my signs again. Then I will probably lie awake, listening to the regular beep of some-one's empty saline bag as their blood is hydrated and kept flowing. In a hospital ward at night life seems suspended, surrendered to machines. Real life happens outside, in the glow of light from the nurses' station where there are thank-you teddy bears and a box of Quality Street, and the soft buzz of talk.

In common parlance, life is often mechanised like this: the peristaltic suction of gullet and guts, the lungs as bellows, the heart as pump. The MRI scanner, slowly surveying the body, draws out sounds like the banging of old iron. A shortage of beds once sent me to a ward of dementia patients, whose minds had wandered off but whose life, bafflingly to them, efficiently ticked on. One patient ate as though she did not know the reason for it. One, defecating on the floor, looked in wonder at the neat piled spiral she had made. One screamed continually at the indignity of bedpans. As for me, so sane as I proclaimed myself, I knocked out my cannula when I washed my hands, and erupted among the quiet visitors spouting blood like a fountain.

Lifeblood. To shed blood is to spill out our existence: which is why the tiniest nick with a kitchen knife, or the prick of a pin, sends such a morbid chill through me. My blood always shocks me with its brightness—surely arterial, even from a scraped knuckle, which splashes, unnervingly, as I scrub the floor. I worry that the thick blue veins in my wrists seem to have moved too near the surface, and try to leave alone the mysterious ancient scratch-scabs that never fall away and simply bleed afresh.

There is sacredness in blood: the vital element in pagan sacrifice, the transubstantiated wine. Priests at Passiontide wear vestments of scarlet, as if to be bathed in it as it flows from the side of Christ. The child-saints I was brought up with, in the shiny shilling booklets that were sold in church, coughed up that arterial blood as they died and were laid to rest among lilies. The blood of Elizabethan martyrs transferred its numinous power to the women who trailed hems in it, and the men who dipped handkerchiefs. In Federico García Lorca's agonised lament for Ignacio Sánchez Mejías, the bullfighter's blood bursts singing from his veins like a nightingale; the poet cannot bear to see it stilled, whether in a goblet or a casket, whether chilled by frost or simply dried on the sand that the attendants rake away.

When talk turns to the sacredness of life, therefore, it is blood that seems to contain it. The gesture of taking someone's pulse, touching the fingers gently to the wrist, then falling silent to listen, always strikes me as holy. So, too, does the stroking of the statue by Pygmalion, willing the lifeblood to flow.

> Soft wax must feel as his stone lover does—
> an amberball long lying in the sun,
> a fire-warmed candle sheltered in the palm
> to take impress of fingers, heart of heat
> glowing along cell walls. So limb by limb
> she loosens, wakens. At the low bedside
> he leaves his bunched unnecessary flowers;
> heavy as marble now his stroking hands.

In contrast, the doctor testing my breathing beats light and hard, as if on a drum. The bellows inflate and deflate satisfactorily, automatically. Neither of us feels the same reverence for inbreath and outbreath. Perhaps we should.

It is not long since Covid taught us to fear breathing: our own, whether too shallow, wheezing, or spasmodic, and especially the virus-filled breathing of others. We shied away as joggers steamed past and, even with masks clamped tight, we tried not to inhale more than necessary. We suppressed our breath, as we suppressed the dance and glance of our expressions and our impulse to touch others. To save life—the government's constant plea—we locked it down.

Li Wenliang was in at the beginning. On December 19, 2019, he put up a post on his social page about an odd cluster of pneumonia cases at Wuhan Central Hospital. As an ophthalmologist, dealing with eyes, he did not normally take much interest in respiratory diseases. In fact, his social page mostly sang the glories of food: Japanese fish rolls with lashings of wasabi, the unmissable chicken drumsticks at the railway station, plates of steaming beef noodles, and the egg pancakes (that wonderful dopamine hit on his tongue!) that got him through his long night shifts. Lurid Instagrams accompanied his reviews. Snacking made him chubby, but he never quite took to sport. Apart from a bit of badminton, he mostly exercised by live-streaming snooker, commenting live on socials and energetically querying the ref's decisions.

The pneumonia cases he had noticed were unexplained but seemed to have their source in the pungent, litter-strewn warren of stalls that made up the local wet market. "Seven cases of SARS . . . ?" he asked. He quickly corrected it—the virus was not yet identified for sure—but, to his horror, his post had already gone viral. It got him into deep trouble, and he was made to sign at the police station a pledge, twice authenticated with his thumbprint in red ink, to stop spreading rumours and disrupting the social order.

Uneasy now, he returned to work. But soon he was in a worse fix. On January 8, 2020, after treating an old woman for acute angle-closure glaucoma, without a mask (since she had no fever), and mingling his breath with hers, he caught the new infection himself. She, too, had run a stall in the wet market. By January 10 he had begun to cough. Food raptures were forgotten now; obsessively his posts tracked the relentless fall of the oxygen levels in his blood. He was an optimistic sort and thought he might be back to full lung function in a couple of weeks; but by late January he could not breathe on his own. From his bed, now on continuous-flow oxygen but with his eyes defiant above the tubes, he continued to put up posts, send emails, and give interviews on socials, whether or not the authorities wanted to hear him—until, at last, breath left him.

When breathing was arduous or dangerous, all life was. The mere buying of bread in the corner shop, the paying for it, the customary to and fro of laughter and conversation, became an expedition to the edge.

March 30, 2020
She of the black hair and bewitching grin,
battering the coffee-maker, bantering
with all the builders from the hospital,
gear swinging at their waists; she who can bawl
her dim lovesick assistant to fill stock
and give the best-befores another check—

now from behind a barricade of chairs
summons the men to bring their crisps and beers
singly and slowly, and with blue-gloved hands
thrusts out the card machine; firmly defends
her counter from their cash, their coughing. Then
the store once emptied out and quiet again
she shrinks, exhales—and suddenly there lies
a shipwreck-light of terror in her eyes.

Every surface swarmed with hazard, but the danger of air
itself was doubly disturbing.

April 9th 2020
They say today
the virus travels
even in speech,
so that the words
we roll around
and quickly pitch

like tennis balls
over to one another
will catch us out—
not in intent
or emphasis
or tangling doubt,

but in sheer
violence of vowels,
sibilants sent

hissing with sickness, hard
consonants that strike
or end
child, parent,
friend.

On April 7 the Prince of Wales, as he then was, celebrated the 250th anniversary of Wordsworth's birth by reading part of "Tintern Abbey" on the radio. His tone was warmly reassuring. The poet, looking down on the abbey ruins, felt

A presence that disturbs me with the joy
Of elevated thoughts; a sense sublime
Of something far more deeply interfused,
Whose dwelling is the light of setting suns,
And the round ocean and the living air,
And the blue sky, and in the mind of man;
A motion and a spirit, that impels
All thinking things, all objects of all thought,
And rolls through all things.

I made a note to reread the poem but wrote beside it: "1,000 people died today." Suddenly, Wordsworth's life breath seemed to be passing us by.

In dead blue calm
we sit wide-spaced
like cormorants on shingle,
watching the sea that breaks
oddly, idly, apart from us

as if what moves in it
and also moves in us
is not the same

while all the grand
unvisited hotels
watch with their blinded windows
the disregarded street
where one sleek cyclist passes
and one quick man
with a silk Italian scarf
clamped to his frightened mouth—

The clustered sycamores
have not forgotten
how to bud, split cleanly
from pink sheaths; the bees
browse as they ever did;
yet what moves in the trees
and also moves in us
is not the same—

Instead of littering
white-petal loveliness
on wind, on grass,
we scatter our contagion,
used tissues, masks.

On April 27 a *fata morgana*, a peculiar light effect invert-
ing the seascape, the wind farm, and the sky, drew us to the

beach. And we remained, as ever, gazing out, intensely aware of breathing together and sitting, or standing, alone.

> Shallow as a lake
> the covid sea
> lies against a bank of sand-light
>> still
>
> and the turbines stand in mist
> of their reflections
>> still
>
> and two small mackerel boats cut their
>> engines
>>> still
>
> and the man
> on his paddleboard and a swimmer
>> still
>
> watch ourselves on the shingle separate statues
>> still

During Covid, a saxophone player used to practise by the sea: a middle-aged Black man, rather shy, with worn clothes and no carrying case for his glittering, glowing horn. When he felt unsure of a piece he would pace in the shadow of the rusting hulk that marked the end of the zip-wire; but when he was confident he would stand on the Banjo Groyne and fling out his notes splendidly, defiantly, as the indifferent water rose and fell. We leaned on the promenade rail to listen, still keeping our authorized distance, so hungry for the sound of music carried on living breath.

When I first came to the coast I thought I might do something similar. I pictured myself at the window with a clarinet, effortlessly playing up the octaves and down again, letting my notes sparkle and ripple with the water. The fact that I couldn't play one was no obstacle, for I could surely manage something moving and simple: a human greeting, like a gull's cry.

Fairly soon I lowered my sights and bought a recorder instead. It was cheap and plastic, the sort any primary-school child could play. But I seemed to lack the breath for it, or the technique, or both. The recorder cried and squawked, as grass-blades used to when I blew them through cupped hands; my fingers stubbed, slipped, missed the holes. After many days I gave up. But I did not put it away. Instead I still keep the recorder on my music pile under the window, lying at an angle, as if at any minute I could take it up and play spontaneously to sea and sky. As if I sometimes actually do.

For a time another potential instrument lay beside it. It was an offcut pruned from an elder tree by my uncle, in his nineties, boldly leaning out from a twelve-foot ladder to slash it away with a billhook. He was too old for this work, he confessed, and the ladder too rickety; he had prudently slung rope under every rung to hold him, lightly springing, if he fell through. The elder twig fell as lightly, already dried hollow: already calling, somehow, for breath to make it live again.

Hard, light, empty as old bone
this length of elder, lopped off
yesterday, begs to be held
and played. It's straight enough
but unholed, therefore without
notes, voiceless. One sharp end
is sliced diagonal, a mouthpiece
possibly; the other's knot-bound,
close-stopped. Yet I sense
there's music in it somehow,
curled, ready, tensed to spring
up, out, as the branch below
the billhook bent, swayed, sang,
and the ladder man
drew back his sweating hand—

I never did make a pipe of it. Had I done, it would have
sung of the copse and of blackbirds; of staining purple
berries, and flowers held to the June sun like saucers of
champagne. Woodwinds and reeds are the voices of wild
landscapes. In their plaintive moods they call up wide
marshes or lonely meadows with no other human soul; in
brighter modes they match arpeggios with the birds. On
walks by the Hampstead ponds I find myself lingering by
stands of reeds, listening as the wind draws out a densely
whispering song. They move as one then, bowing and
rippling like a thin green army, for another part of their fasci-
nation is their closeness to human bodies. The oboe, clarinet,
and cor anglais are so poignant because they risk the vulner-
ability of human breath: its stops, starts, and strugglings, the

way it trembles and breaks. Their hollowness, too, is ours, though they ooze thick sap rather than blood. The reeds by the ponds are as tall as a man, jointed and with white plumes tossing from their heads. One sharp winter morning I met a group of dog walkers beside the first pond, each feathered like the reeds with their own floating breath and each golden, as the sun rose.

From cousins of these comes the most haunting music of all, that made by the Turkish or Persian *ney*, which is all reed. This was the instrument Rumi played and also knew he was resting against God's lips as God breathed deeply through him. And he was not alone. Divine breath continually filled and called each hollow reed in the reedbed of creation, seeking from each human being the life-notes that were theirs.

> God picks up the reed-flute world and blows.
> Each note is a need coming through one of us, a passion,
> a longing-pain.
> Remember the lips
> where the wind-breath originated
> and let your note be clear.
> Don't try to end it.
> *Be your note!*

Neys are famously difficult to play, their long bodies held down and away at an angle from the lips. I would never have mastered either that or the microtones produced from slightly altering the stopping. Probably no sound would have emerged at all. But to Rumi, the *ney* that is my soul would have been singing all the time, remembering the sugarcane sweetness of Paradise while struggling in the world.

The music of the *ney* is an exchange between separated lovers with a single life. It is also an instinctive conversation; as instinctive as that of birds, whose very bodies—from the hard, ridged tongue to the light cage of ribs, like a softly echoing drum—are instruments of music. A lark springing from the meadow moves so hectically, leaping and dipping in ever-wider spirals, that it seems to be controlled by some overhanging power. As it climbs, soon sky-lost, its small wings vibrate frantically, and at the apex it glints in the sun, as though it is another pipe raised and held to the lips of Rumi's unseen Player. The blackbird that perched once on my scaffolding, a sleek-robed chorister with a bright, knowing eye, tried out each new phrase by rehearsing it, repeating it, as if determined to find what his own note was and to perfect it.

Birds large and small build up with song the living scene around them. The finches I disturbed in a winter field were singing the glassy, stiffening frost; as I crossed a wood at twilight, one tawny owl in the high ash trees drew out the dread of night. Linnets sharpen the spines of a gorse bush and its studs of yellow blooms; a robin in a London plane sings the brisk, unsleeping city. A hovering kestrel draws a trembling connection between sky and meadow, and the grunt of a raven rings a vast dry valley with poverty and emptiness.

Doves, too, build up the scene in which they find themselves. I once visited the ruins of an ancient monastery where, though few birds were visible, their gentle coos were re-establishing the place. With a presence scarcely louder than the drift of a feather, they were mortaring the tumbled lime-stone, binding it together in traceried windows and curved stairs, murmuring and making, as the chants of monks in procession would have done. Rumi would have said that was my job too: to remake the world by seeing and singing.

One of the most ancient wind instruments yet found was made from the wingbone of a bird. The maker may have thought that any principal bird-limb was bound to be full of music, but this was no songster. It was a coarse black vulture of the hills, its red naked neck pushed from a ruff of feathers; a bird of following and silent watching. Perhaps the maker hoped this carpal bone would weave shamanic magic and help him fly. Some impetus made him pierce it here and there, then raise it to his lips—as the God of Genesis did when, having thumbed out his man-shape of clay, he blew into the still-closed nostrils and gave him life.

That creative, formative power had already been breathed into sun and moon, waters above and waters beneath, soil and seeds. The divine breath was warm, combining love and fire. In Proverbs and Ecclesiasticus it was personified as Wisdom, a female principle that proceeded from the mouth of God and hovered beside him as he measured out the seas and the skies. When Earth was made, Wisdom covered it like a mist to encourage life to grow. The four winds, too, carried the divine breath hither and thither.

Other civilisations used the same image of breath, whether or not the breather had a human form. It was the *prana* of the Vedas, the *qi* of the Taoists, the *pneuma* of the Greeks, as well as Rumi's longing Player of the flute. It was also the *ha* of the Egyptians, for whom the hidden nature of the divine, the self or soul, was simply breathing. This life force surged equally through atoms and through interstellar space, pervading everything, bringing with it—in the case of humans—knowing and feeling, and binding mind and body together. As Rumi put it, "A wealth you cannot imagine flows through you."

Genesis makes curiously little of that first inspiration. God took Adam, scooped from wet earth, huddled in his hand like an ocarina, and blew. He may have breathed softly, carefully, like a first kiss, or as if to detach a bubble from a wand. Or he may have given short, sharp gasps, as Amazonian shamans rouse people from unconsciousness by blowing leaf powder through a reed. Short, sharp breaths until the patient judders awake, splutters, and cries. Or, perhaps, sings.

In Milton's *Paradise Lost* nothing was known or described in the world that Adam, now alone, woke up to. But directly after he had tested his new limbs by walking and running, he tried out his tongue to see what it could do. Immediately, since God had intended it so, he named the sun, the Earth, the "happie Light," banks "profuse of Flowrs" and "goodliest Trees," from which the Presence Divine, hearing his voice, came out to welcome him. His new, strong throat was now at God's disposal, his hard rib cage another echo chamber. His praise was as constant and instinctive as that of trees leafing or birds chorusing, and one with theirs. Even the morning mists were urged to join him.

Ye Mists and Exhalations, that now rise
From Hill or steaming Lake, duskie or grey,

Till the Sun paint your fleecie skirts with Gold,
In honour to the Worlds great Author rise,
Whether to deck with Clouds th'uncoloured skie,
Or wet the thirstie Earth with falling showers,
Rising or falling still advance his praise.

In this brief, bright interval before the Tempter-Serpent appeared, life, love, and song flowed reciprocally together. Exile from Eden obscured and complicated matters, but in every age some human beings kept the habit going. "I will sing to the Lord as long as I live," said the psalmist; "I will make music to my God while I have my being." A medieval Irish poet echoed him, writing in some glade where nightingales sang the silver rivers and wove the evening trees: "It is folly for any man in the world to cease from praising Him, when the bird does not cease, and it without a soul but wind." The natural response of a created being was to breathe back the breath of the Creator.

Luciano Pavarotti sang in the certainty that his glorious tenor voice was a gift from God. Critics and other singers often called him lazy or undisciplined; he called it doing as he liked with this instrument he had, which packed opera houses the world over and made beautiful women fall at his feet. If he felt out of sorts or peeved with someone, he would naturally cancel the concert booking; just as, if a healthy diet bored him and his girth was fine to his mind, it was back to porterhouse steaks and caviar scooped with a tablespoon.

He was unintellectual, without conservatoire training and barely able to read music. But then reading music was hard and annoyed him; learning from a score, he once said, was like making love by post. Words—even those of "*O sole mio*," every tenor's meal ticket—were hard to commit to memory. In opera or recital he almost never ventured out of his crisp, supple Italian, in which he could say everything he wanted.

Yet he knew what he was doing. He sang purely by instinct, perfectly aware of "how it should go" and trusting that any good conductor could follow him. *Natural* and *effortless* were the words most often applied to his smooth, honeyed, gorgeous voice, which made listeners' skin break out in goose bumps and hairs rise on the back of their necks. "*Lasciare andare*" was his motto: it was there, pour it out, like a wonderful wine. Though he used every sinew in his body to produce his high notes, glistening with sweat and mopping his face with a huge white handkerchief, the voice showed no strain. At the end his smile would be ecstatic, as it was when at the age of four he had jumped on the kitchen table, setting the lamp swinging, to sing "*La donna è mobile*" to his adoring aunts. By his death, he held the world record for curtain calls.

Joan Sutherland, Australia's most celebrated soprano, also believed her voice was given. Whether by God or Nature, she had no idea. It had always been there as she grew up in New South Wales, floating out heedlessly as she washed the plates or wandered around the house. She sang anything: operatic arias, to be sure, but also Uncle Tom's favourite ode to ginger ale, "My old woman's an awful boozer":

And when we was lyin' in bed that night
she went
Pop! Pop! Poppety-pop!

Out in the garden, on the swing under the camphor laurel tree, Joan would sing to the birds, and critics sometimes said later that only the birds could approach her fluting scales. Certainly she was built to sing loud: "no sylph," as she put it, with docker's shoulders, a rock-solid diaphragm and the constitution of an ox. The Voice itself, though, was such a delicate thing. She endured frequent gruelling operations to clear out her sinuses and antrums. It was typical—and a bloody nuisance, in her opinion—that on the opening night of Donizetti's *Lucia di Lammermoor* at Covent Garden in 1959, the highest point so far in her career, she seemed to be getting a cold. Her throat felt tight and dry; a colleague said she should sip hot Ribena between the acts. But once she was on the stage, the Voice took over. Its pure *coloratura* sparkled through her early arias, drawing bursts of applause. In the third act, where Lucia crept downstairs in a nightgown spattered with her husband's blood, it began to trill with incipient madness, to echo itself, to break into exquisitely wild arpeggios and cadenzas, until it soared to a top D-flat of utter despair. The audience erupted then with roars, flowers, and rapture, saluting a new world star. Afterwards, utterly dazed, Joan could only say: "Well, what do you know about that?"

And then there was Miriam Makeba, a South African singer and battler against apartheid, who said she was shy. When Nelson Mandela came in the 1950s to meet the band she sang with, she sat quietly in the corner and let the men do the talking. Years later, when she was introduced to John Kennedy at the White House, she was awed at the thought that "little me," "a songbird," had held the smooth white hand of the president. Her speaking voice was thin, light, and high: really, she thought, just an ant's voice.

All her conditioning taught her to be quiet. She was hushed from her first days, as her mother suckled her in the jail to which she had been sent for illegally brewing and selling beer. Miriam kept her silence as a teenager, nannying and doing chores for whites, who would look at her as if they owned her. It became second nature to slip in and out of scullery doors, holding her breath, doing nothing that whites might find disruptive.

And yet it was plain from her performances that something else was going on. Shy or not, silent or not, she hummed and vibrated like a plucked string. And the tension grew in her as the music did. After a slow saunter onstage, gazing at her high-heeled shoes as if she was still a timid thing, she would suddenly straighten her back, flex her muscles, throw back her head, and let loose an incandescent smile. Her strong, lithe body writhed and shook. Her shoulders hunched, her hips gyrated. Slinky, strutting, wild-eyed, and joyous, Miriam danced as she sang the Friday-night songs of Black Sophiatown, the songs of her life, clicking and clapping the Xosha words. It was natural, she said, for Black South Africans to turn their "cries from the heart" into rhythm and joy. She simply did the same. "Music gets deep inside me," she explained, "and starts to shake things up." When she felt that force, wherever it came from, she had to cry back all the strength, warmth, sensuousness, and burnished beauty of Africa, as well as its songs.

At the start of 2021, still in the second Covid lockdown, I returned to Parliament Hill. Strangely for early March, the days were often foggy, and even simple breathing seemed too hard. Down by the Lido the fog was thick: a damp muffling scarf, a taste of soot in the mouth, a too-close view of cottony, absent fields. On the football pitch the white goal could just be seen, standing in a mess of muddied grass from which three boys, like wraiths, were running and fading away.

Yet further up the hill on the Highgate side, where the tall oaks stand, a tree was coming into being. It grew up through the fog, slowly becoming visible, floating slightly as if in water. In its winter bareness, it might have been an anatomical drawing of the lungs. As I looked at it, I felt my own lungs gradually defining, clearing, filling with breath, and life rising through me from the ground itself, as if the sodden London clay was tunnelled with space and, through the space, power.

> From vapour drifts
> each naked tree
> breathes
> and is breathed
> incrementally,

some as soft
graphite
shaken on paper
some

as faint lungs
arching,
branching
about a heart—

So I stand too
branching
breathed out
and drawing through
as all around
the oak trees do

The path that ran to the top of the hill was lined with blackthorn, a mass of white lace on twigs still spiked and cruel. It might have made a wedding canopy for some barefoot girl, and garlands for her hair. Breath was moving through this too, almost visibly easing open the tightly clustered buds, drawing them out like the flowering of frost on windows. One old, scarred, lichened tree especially moved me, so heavy with this breath that it had fallen across the path. As Rumi would have seen it, it was giving back all the song it could.

There is no perfume to blackthorn. But the old tree reminded me, in its stillness and prodigality, of the rain-soaked lilac bush in a Hampstead garden into which I plunged my face once on a whim, only to find myself bathed in scent that was overwhelming, strong as love, and as demanding. Astonished and almost frightened, I backed away. I needed to respond, but had no idea how. Anyone seeing me might have thought I was retreating from the storm clouds that loomed to the west, fumbling my plastic cape together as the first drops fell. But I was running from a sudden encounter with more life than I could bear.

Up on the hill I felt the same insistence. My chest filled and ached with it. The power that burned as stars and wheeled as galaxies, that moved through the oaks and through myself, was also here, shining in petals that the next strong wind would scatter far away. As Yeats wrote, recording the words of an old Wicklow peasant, "God possesses the heavens— but he covets the world."

That thought has a long history. The gods of Olympus regularly came down in earthly forms, as swans, bulls, clinking showers of coin, to mate with human girls. In the *Iliad* they cannot bear to keep out of the drama of human affairs. In the *Odyssey*, too, they swoop about, drawn no doubt by the dripping fat of oxen sacrificed on almost every shore. Some writers explain Christ's incarnation not as a redemption mission, but as a remote deity's longing to know what earthly life is like. To chew good bread, feel water run down the throat, fry fish on a beach, feel the wrap of longing limbs; to argue, make friends and also lose them; to see red blood seep from a wound and taste its iron on the tongue—life vulnerable. Even to die, at least in the body, as all created things do. Yet the breathing force I sensed among the blackthorn was not personalised. It was simple being, focused power, like the flow of water or air. It came closest perhaps to Rilke's *"Du"*—"You," the intimate pronoun he tremblingly fixed on, rather than engaging too often with that other, loaded word: a pervasive longing that might be encountered anywhere. Rilke explained it as "dark / and like a web: a hundred roots / silently drinking." Others liked to paint their God in gold, surrounded with flames and words of light, but Rilke preferred to use the colours of apple-bark for this vast enigma, hidden and working in the very depths of things. Within that infinite darkness life revealed itself quietly, like a river "mining the silences of stone."

This power could also be skin-close, "a great presence stirring beside me." It was the shadow that fell, like Rumi's bird-shadow, across the pages of a book and made it glow, or "the drifting mist that brought forth the morning." It was the fragrance of the deep soil out of which trees—like those Highgate oaks—rose into existence. Rilke felt it within him, ripening him like a fruit for a simple but astonishing purpose: to be the hands, the ears, and especially the eyes of this life force in the world. For, in that infinite darkness, God was alone. Humanity had to explore creation on God's behalf: closely observe it, experience it, and thus bring it into being as Adam had done. Rilke had to be God's pitcher, watering those hundred roots; God's sandal to tread the Earth, and a cloak to ward off bad weather. In one extraordinary image, of the poet circling God as "a primordial tower," they were almost interchangeable:

I've been circling for thousands of years
and I still don't know: am I a falcon,

a storm,

or a great song?

Rumi's flute player, too, was often simply a phenomenon, a verb rather than a noun: wanting, waiting.

Nor did this power discriminate. It was universal, seeking and needing even the spiked branches, the vague, clammy afternoon, and the faint note of the single bee hovering in the blackthorn flowers. It needed untrained and ordinary lungs, as well as those of superstars; the child shouting in the stroller and the raucous choruses of teenage girls, as well as the voice of the young woman who sat behind me in the Oxford coach, complaining.

On the phone she's loud and coarse.
"Tell you what, yeah, what I found out, yeah,
you know I didn't show up for work today?
They put a star against my name."
There's more. But as the blurred sky pours
down darkness and the sultry air
begins to cool, she sings. Light, far away,
sweet, pure and tender with a wavering flame.
Tell them to put a star against her name.

It seemed that I should sing back myself, there on the hill: sing in my own habitual, snatching fashion, reaching for words and setting them down. After all, I fancied myself a poet, my lips already rimed with baptismal salt as I wandered in the sea air of the Downs. Surely, since poetry was music, that would be good enough.

But somehow it wasn't. I felt obliged, among the oaks and the blackthorn, to add actual music to creation. *Be your note*, Rumi had told me, and the challenge was irresistible: to show that I was there on the hill in the clearing, flowering spring with my own breath to offer, and human music. The problem was how. I had failed at the clarinet and, shamefully, at the recorder too. My throat seemed too tight and embarrassed to sing. All I could manage, almost under my breath, was to whistle a couple of Gregorian phrases that I stifled quickly before anyone heard me.

That failure was especially disappointing. For years I had thought of whistling as my particular music: curls of favourite tunes that then wandered mysteriously away, taking their own paths, or my path. I had taught myself to do it at the age of nine or ten, puffing and blowing in careful imitation of the rough boys on the waste-ground. I whistled when I rode the hobbled bike that someone had abandoned there, and as I climbed the scrappy young trees that swayed alarmingly under me. Girls with good manners did not do any of those things. So whistling became a solitary practice, something for moments of happy aloneness, usually in the open air. It still is.

Anyone hearing it might think it casual. After all, boiler-fixers do it, and builders forgetting the social prohibition to whoop after women, and the dog walkers who call "Bogart!" or "Caesar!" out of the fascinating woods. On that murky afternoon I could hear someone else—a man, I presumed— whistling on the hill amid the commentary of crows. His note was soft-edged, unmetallic, wavering as his steps did; not full-throated like the birds, but hesitant and controlled. I knew it would be the same with me. To whistle is an act of concentration, almost of meditation: gathering round the core of myself and focusing inwards, even as the notes flow out. Instinctively I stand still, as if my body is a tensed reed that can no longer move itself. I am all flute then, set up ready.

An American friend once sent me a Chinese poem about whistling, the "*Hsiao Fu*" by a third-century writer, Ch'eng-kung Sui:

> The secluded gentleman,
> in sympathy with the extraordinary
> and in love with the strange,
> scorns the world and is unmindful of prestige . . .
> He gazes up at the concourse of heaven, and treads the
> high vastness . . .
> Then, filled with noble emotion, he gives a long-drawn
> whistle.

I imagined him with silk robes and high blocked shoes, his hair in a pigtail or pushed under an official's hat, pausing on the path. But no, the poet insists, he is secluded, hiding "in the shade of the elegant charm of tall bamboos," where his transcendent self is responding to the glory of the heavens. His whistle is not a casual "Coo!" but perfect heaven-music; he has joined with a power beyond himself and is able to reorder the world. He begins with the weather: with the note *yu* he can now bring frost, and with the note *shang* autumnal drizzle in springtime. He has made himself as hollow as the tall canes around him, in order to sound the breath beyond. "Be that empty," Rumi says, in his implacable way; be filled with greater life.

The whistler I could hear came into view and passed me, letting his notes fade as though he wanted to disown them. Instinctively I smiled at him from my careful social distance, then felt awkward, too, and mumbled a good morning. He didn't answer. Heath-walkers seldom do.

He was old, rather bent, and had a small panting terrier on a leash. A stick was over his arm and a tabloid newspaper jammed in his pocket. His jacket was worn, and one trouser leg was patched at the knee. I immediately surmised that he had sewn on the patch himself with his red, mittened fingers; that he had the look of a widower about him, and had used a sewing kit he had been given in the army, leaning in close to see under a parchment lampshade. And what did he instantly assume about me, a grey-haired woman standing there with a notebook, also in a threadbare jacket, giving him a foolish smile?

The common mist, and our common breath, was thinning and lifting. Neither of us had managed a clear, resounding note; the world had put us off. Instead we had fallen back, as all casual life-catchers do, on random, obvious details: the knee patch, the white stubble, the pulling, panting dog. I went down the hill with fragments in my notebook of yet another life. But my heart was full of the blackthorn.

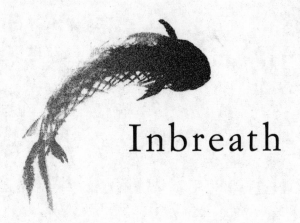

Inbreath

1. Possessing

"WHAT IS LIFE?" CRIED SHELLEY IN 1819; AND wrestled with the thought over many pages before, like everyone else, giving up. This "astonishing thing," this "great miracle," greater even than "the universe of stars, and suns . . . and their motions, and their destiny," refused to be explained. Perhaps in the end it was just the mind perceiving, he volunteered to himself. But what caused the mind to think? And what caused the energy that whirled out of his galvanic machine, making his eyes start from his head and his wild hair stand on end? His last, unfinished poem, "The Triumph of Life," broke off with the same question, but this time with a dash following rather than a question mark: as if it trailed out into the cosmos, still searching.

It is the most persistent mystery, where science gets back to almost the remotest point, almost the first spark, and stops. Steven Weinberg, a Nobel-winning theoretical physicist, devoted a book to the first three minutes after the Big Bang, when in temperatures of thousands of degrees centigrade, a boiling cosmic soup, matter and antimatter continually collided and annihilated each other, before the eventual cooling and settling caused the whole chain reaction of life. But how to explain the ingredients of that first soup, and their spontaneous movement, if it truly was? How to define "time zero" and discern whether there was ever a beginning at all?

Weinberg studied quanta, as well as the cosmos; his equations encompassed both the infinitesimal and the vast. His aim, shared with many colleagues, was to simplify the laws of Nature to one that united all the rest. Yet the further his theories progressed, inwards or outwards, the deeper the mystery became. He managed, at least, to reduce Einstein's four fundamental laws to three, which netted him the Nobel Prize. But he puzzled over the high proportion of dark matter in the universe, a matter with no mass, known only by its effects; and he worried, too, that established quantum theory was inadequate to explain how the tiniest particles behaved. Frustratingly, but intriguingly, their movements seemed influenced by quirks of behaviour and measurement in the scientists observing them, as if—in Shelley's surmise—life was controlled, in part, by minds perceiving.

He was not a man of uncertainty, however. One day the answer was bound to come, whether from the Large Hadron Collider in Geneva or from the four-billion-year-old meteorite that fell in 2021, like a piece of coal from a barbecue, onto a driveway in a quiet suburban street at Winchcombe, in Gloucestershire. The truth might appear in one hundred years; it might also turn up tomorrow. He was certain, in any case, that the cosmos was an indifferent place and its rules implacable. Once that single, possibly life-explaining law was found, there would be no comfort in it. No plan lay behind the universe, let alone a scheme of divine redemption.

Religion made Weinberg furious: not only because it offered no hard evidence for its claims, but because it obstructed the search for truth. Life, he had concluded, was essentially a tragedy, where humans found that every question, even if answered, led inexorably to another. But they had to go on asking. That was human nature.

James Lovelock's most famous hypothesis also began with a question. Was there life on Mars? If so, what were the signs of it? A cosmic traveller viewing Earth, especially a chemist like himself, could tell there was life there from the disequilibrium of gases in the atmosphere. In fact everything associated with Earth—its rocks, trees, seas, atmospheres and life itself—made one self-regulating and self-sustaining whole. He called it Gaia, after the Greek goddess of the Earth. Sometimes, carried away by the satisfying beauty of the system, he called it "she," as if the Earth itself were alive.

But no, he insisted, it was not. Nor, he found, could he get any closer to defining what life was. He could describe it, very technically and soberly, as a program installed in Gaia's operating system. It occurred in any place with an abundant flow of energy; but that might apply equally to flowing streams, hurricanes, and flames. No rational explanation could distinguish self-organising inorganic systems from life. It was also "an almost utterly improbable event with almost infinite opportunities of happening. So it did."

Reason, however, did not always have the last word. As a Quaker by upbringing, Lovelock acknowledged a "still, small voice" within him. It was this that conveyed the ideas that came to him in the small hours and were modelled in his head, three-dimensionally, over breakfast. It was this that pricked his long, wondering coast walks with possibilities of new creations. Armed with these he would go to his workshop-lab, with its lathe, hand tools, and milling machine, its shelves of chemical reagents and homemade equipment, and set to work. Rational thinking played a part, of course. But it was that more powerful, unconscious force, intuition, that sometimes allowed him to grasp "a tiny, sparkling fragment of reality."

Both he and Weinberg might have sighed over the two middle-aged women I saw camped outside the railway station in Newhaven, guarding their display of Jehovah's Witness magazines. The cover headline, above a photograph of the blue, vital, fragile Earth seen from space, was that old question: How had life begun? But it was raining, and there was no discernible trade. From my dry upper deck, I snatched them in passing.

> Neat in a rack they've ranged their magazines:
> "Was Life Created?" Now they wait, ensconced
> hard by the level-crossing, hoods rammed up,
> navy-and-blue umbrella firmly conched
> to windward. Life goes by infrequently,
> God-made or uncreated; no one's drawn
> by the old puzzle; though on that slow train
> a youth sits wondering why he was born.

Midway through his own musings on life, however, Shelley had a sudden run of clarity. He remembered how, as a child and sometimes later, he had felt as boundless as the universe and one with it: running with the west wind, following streams to a source that seemed to lie within his own mind, sketching the companionable sadness of trees. An "unusually intense and vivid apprehension of life" caught him up completely. "Those who are subject to the state called reverie," he wrote, "feel as if their nature were dissolved into the surrounding universe, or as if the surrounding universe were absorbed into their being. They are conscious of no distinction." It was all one, life entire.

Sadly, that feeling became rare. Shelley could put no timescale on it; it simply seemed that, in living, he lost the sense of miracle. Wordsworth, in his "Immortality Ode," was more exact. It was at the age of six that a child was the "best Philosopher," captivated by projects and "new-born blisses," powered with "heaven-born freedom" until school, like a prison-house, closed round him. At that age, or near it, Lovelock received a wooden box one Christmas containing a bell, a torch bulb, wires, batteries, and all kinds of electrical odds and ends, which spurred both questions and experiments. Weinberg, too, inherited from a cousin at six a chemistry set that would, he knew, unlock every secret in the world. And with that came a wonder, which, despite his pessimistic convictions, never left him. "I know that I am mortal and the creature of a day," he would say, quoting Ptolemy, his forerunner in ancient Greece: "but when I search out the massed wheeling circles of the stars, my feet no longer touch the Earth . . . I take my fill of ambrosia, the food of the gods."

The child I was, from around six to ten, could recognise both states: a world of fixed grown-up limits, but also a universe of marvels where my questioning and venturing surged on. In the first state there were rooms I did not enter, cupboards I was not to open, books and precious ornaments that belonged to other people. Rules were attached like labels to every part of life. On visits from the London suburbs to my Kentish great-aunts my manners were closely monitored, from the proper wiping of my shoes on the mat ("Not like a little puppy dog!"), to my sitting, back straight, on the edge of a chair; from the progress of my knife towards the butter, to the passing of the jam and my chewing with polite, closed mouth. For smart occasions I was kitted out with white lace gloves and a hat like a helmet, tight across the brow. Even in bed I felt my aunts' strictures in the feather-pricking eiderdown, the smell of camphor balls and the icy slide of the sheets, as my small feet probed for the stone hot-water bottle wrapped in a cast-off stocking; even in the bathroom they came to check that I ran three tepid inches of water, and no more.

Yet none of this oppressed me. However circumscribed I was in every social way, in thinking, reading, and exploring I was free, and almost every object I encountered possessed a numinous power. I could raid the pile of old books I found in the cupboard under the roof, transfixed as much by the gauzy lithographs as by the stories, and open the carved wooden casket on the chest of drawers to find a tiny pencil, mounted in silver and turquoise in a bracelet, which I did not take, but presumed would be mine as soon as my love was known. Merely by looking at it perhaps I could claim it, as well as the notebook of thin ivory sheets that hung on a tassel beside it, scratched with the remains of magic words. But ordinary things were magical too: the bomb-cracked birdbath in which sparrows sprayed each other, the aromatic settle in the hall, the minute pantry window that opened onto a full green sweep of lawn.

> Cold has a smell.
> The pantry door
> confines it close;
> one small mesh pane
> rebuffs a rose;
> worn tiles put on
> its shining cloak,
> black hanging hams
> add salt and smoke,
> and one wide bowl
> holds it, a skim
> of almost-water
> under cream.

For long spells I was left blissfully alone, as the house was relentlessly cleaned and the garden pruned. Undisturbed, I could sit for hours on the rockery step inventing miniature cities out of moss, shells, and stones; I could read books with the cold Moon, shivering in my nightdress as she rose above the hedge and bleached the bedroom boards white as paper. Out of my aunts' gaze I could run down the lane to a place they did not go, a footpath along the side of the wood (owned and stalked by curious crows), which ended in a little meadow fringed with elder trees and, in spring, more shining cowslips than I had ever seen. A small-gauge railway ran through, now going nowhere, and a rusted engine leaned into the bank. Clambering there one day to check the fogged-up dials that had once recorded speed and steam, I found three precious orchids furred like bees. This was my world, and I was king of it. To quote Wordsworth again, "I saw one life, and felt that it was joy."

The old Kentish word *anointed*, still used by my aunts to describe me when they were much exasperated, summed up my condition well. It sounded holy, obedient; but it meant "trouble." When, decades later, I tried to make a poem-alphabet of my childhood from those disappearing dialect words, it began with the anointed child speaking.

> These are my holy shoes.
> They slide past cracks in paving stones
> with a slither
>
> of unscratched soles. And these
> are holy gloves, string-boned
> between thumb and finger
>
> to hold stiff prayers.
> So now I can't climb trees, catch
> speckled minnows, lick ice cream
>
> from paper, beat down conkers, jump the stairs
> until my ankles sing, sneak through
> thick-nettled gates—can't seem
>
> to live but tightly, rightly.
> Still, I'm free
> to fall into the sea—

In this world the north wind ("Boneless," in the Kentish corruption of "Boreas") was my familiar, a rough intruder in my aunts' house who dared—dared!—to disorder everything.

We called you Boneless, since no wall or set of doors
could keep you out—
you found each bomb-crack, sprang from stocking-drawers,
made chimneys shout—

Lived by the stove, to lick the green enamel pans
like some spoiled pet,
shivered past tea-towels on the airing fans
(no, not dry yet—)

Set Aunt M coughing as she rinsed the cups and spoons,
ash dangled long,
trailing and whining through the hoovered rooms
your boneless song—

But these must be your bones, inch-thick, where
      mallards stalk
with dumb surprise,
these too, white ridges ploughed along the chalk
at cold sunrise,
and these, frost-stencils everywhere we walk,
frost-stems before our eyes.

I understood what the wind and the sea were saying, and what birds quarrelled over. In old Kentish, a "rookery" was "a quarrel with many words."

Up in their roosts
the rooks are arguing,
though not as humans do
hurting during and after,
but as the sea does
rolling and rolling,
not remembering,
or as the wind does
shaking their high nests, then
stroking, whispering
it didn't mean a thing

In this world the turf paths were laid down like carpets especially for me, and every flower and plant was useful to me, as well as to the curious strangers I was forever instructing.

Raked from the just-mown lawn
a feathery mound expands,
never to be rolled in,
greening knees and hands—
But mixed with dandelion
in a small black frying pan
it will delight a half-starved
traveller from distant lands—
such food he understands.

The Sun was another being much like me, ordered with swift tugs of the curtains to leave the smoky lounge and settle down when his bright, loud rays obscured the television; or spoiling our hiding games with careless behaviour.

The shout's out—
seeker turned three times
eyes shut, we scatter
over the steep field, scout
for bushes, hollows, lines
of hedges good and better
to wrap us into, leaf
our too-white legs, mask
panting mouths—here's this,
low, hawthorn, tough
to wrestle under, crouch down
mouse-small in crowdedness
of snag and scratch,
safe though—till through one side
lattice-light-pushing Sun
thrusts in, will show too much,
clearly has never tried
to learn how this is done—
run, hide, seek, hide, find,
leave alone.

And, with the right equipment, I could do magic. The
equipment included a tiny blue tin of foreign coins, an oak
apple polished in my pocket until it shone, a periwinkle shell
lined with mother-of-pearl, and a slim white stick. I still have
all of them except the stick, which had to be fresh-made.
Each one was picked out from the leaf-litter and carefully,
painfully stripped of its close bark with a thumbnail. Ideally
it would have no scars or warts, for those might hobble the
spells. The chosen one would make a proper "shining-stick,"

the Kentish word for the branches young men used to hold up in the marketplace to show they wanted work. As it emerged reluctantly from its sheath of bark, a shining-stick would be slightly damp, newborn, delicate, and bendable, like the bone of a bird. I would hold it up, ritually, to see what it pointed to and where it would take me; for it was master as well as servant now, like other sticks I knew.

> He comes tapping, the poor blind man,
> eyes sunk back deep, and a look
> turned ever upwards and in—
> but his brisk white stick knows the lane
> with a swing and a tap, as well
> as I with my wide eyes can—
>
> And I learned just so to read a book,
> listening and chanting to the prim
> quick raps of a bamboo cane
> over letter-cards glued to the wall—
> to eat the Apple, fire the Gun,
> try on the Hat, shoo off the Rook,
> tap and know the world for sure.
> That's what sticks are for.

I had thrones in this world: on top of the coal bunker, where I read my encyclopaedia; and an old stump near the aunts' house on which, cross-legged, I owned the wood. I also owned each tree in it, the purring wood-doves in them, the beech-mast and acorn cups and the perfect, grass-lined nests made by blackbirds, as smooth inside to my searching hand as my blue tin globe of the Earth. To be hurt was always a surprise, for I was invulnerable, whether jumping for unreachable blackberries or falling from swings; until I hit the scorching gravel, I was as likely to fly. The sea was a friend I would run to and embrace, all of it welling tremendously in my arms. Or, you could say, my soul swelling to contain it.

The Romantics assumed that school would ruin this. For me, education was part of my power, awakening far more than it suppressed; and it went on doing so, except for two hard years when puberty derailed me. At primary school, although I was often made to stand in the corner in the wastepaper basket for talking or giggling, I used the time to chip a map of the world out of the nasty brown paint. Inedible lunches could be smuggled out in a pocket, and the warm, slightly curdled breaktime milk fed to the huge, strange bush with poisonous spots under the cloakroom window. We formed stiff lines for everything in order of height, but thrilling bells summoned us to jump up and rush around, each year up more important stairs to rooms of better books. There were secret doors everywhere, through one of which a bent old woman in a print dress would sometimes appear and then retreat again, as though daylight was not her time. I found secret messages on scraps of paper, built camps in the games field, and saw, through the high closed windows, just enough sky to entertain me before the stinging ruler intervened.

Above all I learned to read, swiftly, voraciously, feeling new texture and consequence all around me. I was staggered that letters alone—those shapes I struggled to fit between the lines in dull, ordinary rows—could convey the thickness of porridge and the prick of a pin in Beatrix Potter's *The Tale of Pigling Bland*, or the smell of a veal-and-ham pie in *The Pie and the Patty-Pan*, or the terrifying pain of the knotted string that tied up Tom Kitten. I made a science of looking for letter-code in unexpected places, on leaves, on chairs, in water-worn rock and in glass, as if each thing was already impregnated with the story of itself.

My second great discovery at primary school was stranger, but also indelible. It was of consonance and beauty, though I knew neither of those words. In the general wax-crayon box I found unimagined colours, especially extra-rare stumps of mauve-blue, with which I immediately fell in love. With the mauve-blue I had to pair, urgently, pink and turquoise. Their stubby grubbiness didn't matter. I knew those were mine, and I would run to the box like a demon to claim them. If one of the three went missing, the cadence they seemed to make together vanished too.

Out of school, that same mauve-blue entranced me to the point where I covered all the blues in my storybooks with a faint violet mask. One watercolour picture of women gathering plums pleased me so intensely, with its gamut of misted blues and purples in golden leaves, that I kept it close and took long doses regularly, like a medicine. Deep into adulthood the haunting went on, whether in the bloom on sloes, or the delicate chicory flowers which, when picked, died within hours, or the chalk-blue paper that lined apple crates and turned grey-white before September ended. That particular beauty seemed essential to me. Believers in synaes-thesia, musical colours, might have said it was a note of a sort

(G-minor, I liked to think). At any event, decades later in a
Welsh orchard I saluted it again.

> Wild plums have fallen in the grass,
> rounded, soft-skinned. We scratch them up
> with plastic tines, first picking out
> the wrinkled or white-spotted ones,
> bending towards our thoughts as day
> thickens to sweetness and decay,
> a vesper-hush. And suddenly
> a picture in a childhood book
> of women gleaning under trees
> dusk-blue and purple shadowings
> chimes like a chord, and I am there
> gathering the colours of the air.

I was fascinated, too, by other affinities: the look of dark-
brown sugar in a willow-pattern bowl, and the way it shifted
damply against a silver spoon; the quiet settling of shucked
peas in a colander, and of fading ash in a fire; the exact sup-
ple fit of a gold-tooled leather lid over a red leather box; the
proper placing of primroses in a little brown jug, and of vio-
lets in a crystal glass. Whenever I encountered or arranged
these things I seemed to hear the sound of rightness, like a
note from far away. This was how it should be done, and not
otherwise. This is how it is. Years later, indoors or out, I still
heard it.

> Once more this impulse to bring everything
> into concordance: instantly to tie

119

blood-berried hawthorn to the storming sky
that broods behind, while field-blown finches fling
into a springing wind the very notes
that live inside it. Our quick minds do this,
though our backs ache; we aggregate our bliss,
feeling our angel wings beneath our coats.

I also knew that the world was not always reliable or, necessarily, real. That girl in the mirror, for example, with the faraway stare and a big white ribbon planted on the wrong side of her head, was not truly me living and breathing, but a version of me that did things clumsily and backwards. She was a copycat who could not read my mind. I could trick her, and with two sweeps of the side-mirrors I could shut her out, this dull, disconcerting creature, and return to myself.

My head was full of tales in which people were turned to stone, carriages to pumpkins, princes to frogs, and vice versa. If wands or magic ointment were laid on scoffers' eyes, they saw fairy processions weaving and sparkling through the grass, and poisonous ragwort flowers turned to gold. When the ointment wore off I felt desperate for them, blind again to a world that really was. I so longed to find treasure lying about me that I would take my present treasures—doll's-house groceries, holy medals, painted glass beads—and throw them out, eyes shut, over the garden, for the sheer joy of possibly discovering them again.

In one story that was read to us, a girl blew a dandelion clock until it reached thirteen. At that, the world she knew became somewhere else. I was fairly unconcerned that the solid scene around me could unravel with such a little breath.

I did that trick whenever I wrote "The Earth, The Universe" at the end of my address, feeling my house and street whirl away to a blurry dot among the stars. The chill that crept in the back of my neck was fascination, not fear. Perhaps I could try the dandelion experiment too, and find myself in new lands. They were not so far away, starting just past the railway bridge or at the top of the lane. I would wrap up bread and cheese in a handkerchief on a stick, as all wanderers did, though I was sure I would always find food if necessary; for this was still my world.

> That nip that Aunt M does
> to cut through thread
> or I to bite out honey
> from a clover-head
> I could use now,
> rabbit-toothed, on this seed
> hard as a jeweller's stone
> to make believe it's bread.

Laboriously and importantly, I would put on my lace-up shoes. But I wouldn't take a map, just my grandfather's precious little compass in its steel case, floating towards due north and containing, in its orbit, everywhere else.

The only instruction I needed was on an oval piece of paper glued inside the lid:

> To render
> this compass luminous at
> night, it should be exposed to

the daylight, or preferably by
burning about 1 in. Magnesium
Ribbon close to the
dial.

And I took that simply because it seemed all travellers should; because, of course, I would immediately know the land I was looking for.

The voices of children are not petulant, but certain. Like birdsong, their play-shouts are clear, natural, and unmodulated, full of carrying power. They, too, like birds, can build up a scene and hold it suspended. One freezing winter afternoon, just before sunset, the chants of children in a far valley seemed to tether the scarlet sun within a cage of trees, slightly swaying, and command it to delay. On a beach, children's voices are the inrush and outflow of the sea, and the glittering web that tempts to the horizon.

Time and again, some incident in childhood is the key to a career. For Karlheinz Stockhausen, a notably percussive composer, it was the sounds his little wooden hammer made as he toddled round the family farm, striking pipe and stove and bucket, no two bangs exactly alike. For Michel Roux, a master-chef, it was standing at his mother's hip as she softly beat up egg whites for a *blanquette de veau*. For Thich Nhat Hanh, the father of "mindfulness," it was a draught of water, on a school trip, from a natural well: an elemental shock of pureness and coldness that he recognised, even then, as the blessing and force of the present moment, unburdened by future or past. Because for very young children, too, there is no time: only now, a moment constantly reencountered and repossessed.

Some lives also reach their fullest expression in childhood. There is a certainty and boldness then that never comes again. Shirley Temple, for example, the world's top-earning film star in the late 1930s, was no exploited moppet, forced into Hollywood by a pushy mother. She did not cry once the cameras were off or complain that her feet ached; no thin-lipped governess marched her up to bed. She loved every moment of it, from her mother's nightly fixing of her fifty-six ringlets in paper, gently repeating her next day's lines meanwhile, to her sailor outfit in *Captain January*, in which she could sidestep and jump like a veteran. It was wonderful fun to play croquet with Orson Welles and do colouring-in with Gary Cooper; to be passed round, at 20th Century Fox, from lap to lap like a mascot; to be given a miniature Oscar, as she was in 1935, and to have her own little bungalow on the studio lot, with a rabbit in a pen and a swing in a tree.

It was true that while making her *Baby Burlesks* at the age of three she was sent several times to the punishment box, which was dark and had only a block of ice to sit on. But that taught her discipline, so that by the age of four she would always "hit the mark"—and, at six, she could match the great Bill "Bojangles" Robinson tap-for-tap down the grand staircase in *The Little Colonel*. She had a bodyguard and a secretary who in 1934 was answering four thousand fan letters a week, but when Shirley wanted to be a tomboy, she was. In the presidential garden at Hyde Park she hit Eleanor

Roosevelt on the rump with her catapult, for which her father spanked her.

Grouchy Graham Greene mocked her as "a complete totsy," but no one watching her five different expressions while eating a forkful of spinach in *Poor Little Rich Girl* doubted that she could act. Her dimpled face could do joy, puzzlement, and pathos within seconds of each other, and most of all determination, jutting out that elfin chin. No grown-up told her there was a Depression on, but she loved to make people happy, so she naturally counteracted it. She grinned from the special Wheaties box and bowl, recommended Lux soap and Packard cars, and made a pretty doll in a polka-dot dress for other sadder little girls. "I don't like to do negatives," she said when she was older. She never did, and the smile that Americans flocked to see was of a child completely at ease in the world she commanded.

That certainty also marked Irving Milchberg, who as a boy in the Warsaw ghetto knew precisely what to do to keep his family going. It involved a lot of running. First, he had to dodge the Polish boys, who would try to beat him up. Then, after 1939, it was the Germans, who built a high wall right in front of his five-floor tenement building (over two hundred families all crammed together, Zionists and socialists arguing, men chanting Torah, parcels being delivered, *rugelach* cooking) to shut off the Jews and starve them to death. But no one could keep in nippy "Itzi" for long.

A small, scratched photograph, worn at the edges, was the only boyhood image I had of him. In that picture, his arm draped familiarly round the shoulders of his good friend Conky, he was all confidence, cockiness, and guile. He knew how to sprint out of the ghetto gate with the work patrols every morning and, before the *gendarme* could raise his rifle or the Polish policeman could catch him by the scruff of the neck, he'd be gone, vanishing into the streets on the Aryan side.

Itzi had business to organise there. He would scavenge carrots, potatoes, or a piece of bread and smuggle them back for the scrubbed-out laundry kettle his mother kept simmering on the stove. Relatives and neighbours would come by for a spoonful of that soup from up and down the building. He was their supplier. Secondhand clothes were easy to scrounge—the men on the work patrols sometimes gave him their worn, sweaty shirts—and he would sell them or swap them for food at whichever market stalls offered the best price. With his light-brown hair and blue eyes, he could easily pass for Aryan and close his deals. His motto was "Buy reasonable, sell better." Three times the Germans got him; three times, by scaling fences or casually climbing off trains, he escaped being shipped to Treblinka. Nothing deterred him. When the ghetto was razed, he organised a little gang of Jewish urchin-orphans on the Aryan side who sold cigarettes outside the tram terminus. He learned, too, how to mend shoes. He never did much thinking, he said; he was simply lucky. But he survived and thrived in this world as if he, and not the Germans, was the one in charge; and as if someone had assured him, personally, that he had as many lives as a cat.

Other children, equally confident, were not so lucky. Perhaps the saddest obituary I have written was for Qusai Abtini, a fourteen-year-old boy who was killed by a sniper during the siege of Aleppo in 2017. He was the star of a TV comedy show in which children played adults; his role was as Abu Abdou, the father of a typically struggling Syrian family. This patriarch would trudge home at night in his blue overalls, throw a bag of shopping at his wife, Umm Abdou, and order her to cook supper; more mellow afterwards, he would lounge on the sofa in his white *dishdasha*, picking his teeth and patting his stomach, occasionally stroking an imaginary beard, while Umm Abdou wailed about the frustrations of her day. Then, after an affectionate put-down, he would waddle off. Every adult foible was exactly observed; and only the occasional too-broad bucktooth grin, or an unprofessional glance to camera, would betray the fact that patriarch Abu Abdou was a child.

He was one of around one hundred thousand children, roughly one-third of the population, in the eastern part of Aleppo, which for months and years had been fought over by the forces of Bashar al-Assad and the Syrian rebels. Thousands had died. For Qusai, as for his friends, school had become intermittent and street football too dangerous; instead he spent hours indoors, watching TV when the power was on and reading, by candlelight, when it was not. He had been recruited from the Abdulrahman Ghaafiqi School, where he had started acting in the seventh grade, by opposition activists, who aired his show on a rebel channel.

All the filming took place in Aleppo's Old Town, through ancient archways and narrow streets with cast-iron window-grilles. But the child actors also scurried past piles of rubble and burnt-out cars, and on-set the sound of shelling and close explosions sometimes made everyone jump. Qusai's job was to keep Aleppans smiling, despite it all. His elder brother had joined the Free Syrian Army, and he himself had played a rebel soldier in a school play, as well as shouting loudly in demonstrations; though when, as Abu Abdou, he briefly joined the rebels himself, he was ambushed by Assad's men and limped home with a bandaged head.

In short, the worlds of comedy and real war were increasingly colliding. And Qusai was getting too old to play a child playing a man. Off-camera he went round in camouflage trousers and a hoodie now, to disguise how young he was. As I wrote about him, I kept before me a photograph of him in his dressing room, where in a battered mirror he brushed his thick hair and practised a slightly pouting smile. Around him the walls had been cracked by shelling, and naked wiring hung from the switches. In his mind he was clearly already a man, a different one, who was sometimes a celebrated rebel fighter and sometimes a film star. Or, perhaps, both. There were no limits to what he could be. The world—even this world of ruins—was all his. It contained Damascus and, beyond that, Hollywood, with its cameras and red carpets and the handprints of the stars.

Then the sniper raised his rifle and saw through the sights a driver making for the only open checkpoint in the city, with a boy beside him. Qusai had been, at one level, just another too-small body placed quickly in the ground. He had also been invulnerable, dreaming, boundless, and what he was then could surely never die.

2. Seizing

ON A BRIGHT SPRING MORNING ON HAMPSTEAD Heath, I met a young man standing sentinel under a tree. The tree was a stately horse chestnut just breaking into leaf, and he stood admiring it, gazing up into it, shading his eyes to see better. He wore shabby artist's clothes and a woolly hat daubed with white paint, like a nimbus. In a bag on his shoulder was a sketchbook; with a reverent unlatching of clasps, he opened it for me. It was full of exquisite pencil sketches of jackdaws and crows, but these were merely "copied off the internet"; his real delight was to draw day by day, also in pencil, the budding and leafing of this tree.

It had long been a favourite of mine too. Horse chestnuts were the first trees I had regularly looked up into (musing where to direct my stick to bring down conkers), to see the branches mazing and layering like a shifting, silent city. This particular one I had sometimes sheltered under, not keeping very dry, but sensing the rough trunk as a steady friend, breathing warmth into me. In the ambit of this tree, or rather its embrace, I felt pulled into another world.

That morning the new leaves, deep-cut at their long

edges, hung down like light-green satin pinked with shears. I mentioned it in passing. "You can't see a thing," the artist said quietly, "until you draw it, and get into the life of it. Between the tiniest particles, subatomic particles, there is movement. And we don't know what that movement is." He began to draw, and I left him, as one might leave a person who has fallen into trance.

Wordsworth described that feeling, when

> . . . with an eye made quiet by the power
> Of harmony, and the deep power of joy,
> We see into the life of things.

In such "serene and blessed" moods, he wrote, "we are laid asleep / In body, and become a living soul."

Tennyson, too, recorded this. He was out walking, perhaps on the Isle of Wight, perhaps in the swirling black cape and wide-brimmed hat of his public persona, when he picked a flower out of a wall. It might have been yellow saxifrage or pink herb-Robert with its lacework leaves, a tiny wisp of a thing.

> Flower in the crannied wall,
> I pluck you out of the crannies,
> I hold you here, root and all, in my hand,
> Little flower—but if I could understand
> What you are, root and all, and all in all,
> I should know what God and man is.

He would grasp what life was. But, understandably, he drew back from the immensity of that idea. Some decades earlier Coleridge had done the same, so moved by the sight of a single daisy blooming in March that he pledged never to pick a flower again: never to snap that shred of consciousness, that thread of life. The poet-watchman, gazing nervously into the mystery-filled dark, a tiny flower curled in his fingers, cries "*Qui vive?*" "Who lives?" and finds that everything does.

For Seamus Heaney, tools and implements lived. His hands, big, red, and with squared-off nails, were not those of a poet. They had paid out rope in long loops, feeling the strain in each fibre of it; they had dressed a hay-ruck and combed it down with a pitchfork that tossed, pressed, and probed with its delicate double tines.

> Riveted steel, turned timber, burnish, grain,
> Smoothness, straightness, roundness, length and sheen,
> Sweat-cured, sharpened, balanced, tested, fitted.
> The springiness, the clip and dart of it.

His hands had felt the tug and strum of a fishing line in a river, coming alive of itself as the trout nudged it, and the whispering of a green silk cast through the air, "saying *hush* / And *lush*, entirely free . . ." He liked to work with the heavy spade, slicing and nicking the turf with its clean plate-edge, and with the "lightness and rightness" of a rake. As for the sledgehammer, with its gathered force, it "so unanswerably landed / The staked earth quailed and shivered in the handle."

When he moved to poet-work, his pen (a faithful Conway Stewart, guttering and snorkelling its full draught of ink) became another tool with which he dug into both the white paper and the bottomless "sump and seedbed" of the earth. From this he drew a crop of words that "felt like its own yield," heavy in the hand, to be widely sown in any place where people were disposed to listen. In his world, the most prosaic things deserved his steady gaze. Crocks in the dairy "spilled their heavy lip of cream"; the old settle bed was "cargoed with / Its own dumb, tongue-and-groove worthiness"; fresh-sawn boards lay "spick and span in the oddly passive grass"; his hand-sewn satchel and old leather football both lived and sang. There was nothing, not the least "dead" twig thrown in the hearth to hiss and spit at the ashes, that did not declare its being and move towards action.

In another part of Ireland, Eavan Boland saw that inward life through a woman's eyes: all women's eyes, in a land where they were largely excluded from both the history and the literature. Their stories were untold, confined to home and garden-plot, childbearing, and night feeding, and when great events unfolded they were never "on the scene of the crime." Dim bedrooms where skirts hung over chairs, or close steamy kitchens with kettles jigging, were their setting. Yet in hers, as if complicit in enslavement, the cups winked; trays waited to be taken down; a silver ladle, making its "smooth / Mimicry of a lake," bent and shone:

> . . . and in its own
> Mineral curve an age-old tension
> Inches towards the light.

Windows whitened her room, and as she left it a shawl swung over her shoulders, flinging out its scent. Even here, the poet shared her agency with a piece of woven cloth.

In St. Lucia, Derek Walcott's pen was a Caribbean swift, a type of sea-dipping Hermes "leaping the breakers, this dart of the meridian," crossing and recrossing the waters like memory:

> She could loop the stars with a fishline, she tired
> porpoises, she circled epochs with her outstretched span;
> she gave a straight answer when one was required.

At other times his seizing pen was a long egret's beak, "plucking up wriggling insects / like nouns" from a mangrove swamp; or a crab, "obliquity burrowing to surface." Without that sea life in it, glittering round his home island, his nib pushed "through a thick nothing." His blue portable typewriter also summoned him each morning, after cigarette and coffee, to walk like a lithe-limbed fisherman "towards the white noise / of paper," and set out on it in his hollow oared pirogue. That craft, too, the *In God We Troust* of his epic poem *Omeros*, ached and strained from the shore like the god-built and god-directed *Argo*, taking him where it would. On board, he fished up live images: a smooth white beach-stone became a woman's supple breast, and linen sheets rose and fell, even on an empty bed, as if waves or lovers were in them.

The best poets catch life by losing all boundaries between what they observe and themselves. Stanley Kunitz, once America's Poet Laureate, "stretched into bird" to overfly his childhood country around the Quinnapoxet River, casting his brief shadow over the land and the road that "tried to loop me home." Earlier, as he read in *Time* about the Pacific salmon, he felt himself becoming a fish. The words began to flow and he followed them, coiling through life, slipping out of his skin,

> nosing upstream,
> slapping, thrashing,
> tumbling
> over the rocks

He had the sense of swimming underwater "towards some kind of light and open air that will be saving":

> Becoming, never being, till
> Becoming is a being still.

Kunitz's sense of poetry-making was almost an animal instinct; as soon as he could feel his own "interior rhythm" in what he observed, whether slithering fish or falling leaf, he knew the poem would work. He never doubted that instinctive empathy, for everything was one life; to touch any part of the web of creation was to make the whole tremble. In his last years, confined to his seaside garden in Rhode Island through which he slowly wandered, his only wish, he said, was to become language itself: pure rhythm and describing, pure words.

Les Murray, the towering poet of Australia, practised the same alchemy. As a farm boy he spent so much time around cattle that, with no trouble, he could share their "hull-down affinities," their "curveting, fish-leaping" when anxious, even the "puffed felt" of their manure. Yet his barns lived too, "thin with frosted straw," and his cornfields, "decaying / to slatternly paper." The dead rabbits he dropped into his burlap bag were still straining to escape him. On a greater dare, he also dug down into the dry scrubby earth to "translate" the voices of animals and plants: the "me me me" dew-flash of finches in seed grass, or the rasp of a cockspur bush, "sharp-thorned and caned, nested and raised, earth-salt by sun-sugar." Words were the rifle bullets with which he bagged what he saw, like the rainbow rosellas in the trees or the playing cards he could split edge-on; and the arrival of a poem was a physical thing, a tickle in the cerebrum, his muscles tensing until, like Kunitz, he was "inwardly dancing" with the onrush of life.

So it is for the great ones. Lorca declared, in the first book he published, that he was interested only in "the interiors of things." It was a prose book of wanderings through the dryness of Castile, Leon, and Avila, a form he abandoned soon enough for the risky excavations of poetry. No vaulted cathedral or gorge-gouging river could compare with the depths he then leapt into, his flesh sliced by lilies, stretcherbeds breaking into carnations, the moon transformed into the horns of wading cattle, while the weed-green water in stone cisterns "blossomed into silence."

Rilke, too, in his *New Poems*, became a supple panther pacing at the Paris zoo, his world cross-hatched and shuttered by the iron bars of his cage; he inhabited the turning marble of an ancient torso of Apollo, radiating light from all its surfaces;

and he entered the moving stillness of a bowl of roses, end-
lessly filling that space until everything was contained there:

> the world outside, the wind and rain, the patient
> spring, the guilt, the unrest, muffled Destiny,
> the darkness of the Earth at evening,
> the wanderings, the migrations of the clouds,
> and energies which drift from distant stars . . .

> The roses hold it all, content, within them.

The scope of those interiors is astonishing. They seem,
as Rilke said, to contain all there is. Under the rind or the
skin, even within the stone, lie gulfs of vertiginous space, shot
through with vivifying fire, from which faint explorers like
myself instinctively retreat. Sometimes every object thrums
with this huge inwardness, a life and consequence beyond
itself. I have felt it in the steel-straight perspective of rail-
way tracks, the pothole ice that shatters into perfect stars, the
broken traceries of a hedge in which a jackdaw pauses, and
the setting down of cut chrysanthemums on a stone floor; in
the wooden reels round which I wind cotton thread, and the
needle-eye that dodges my attempts

> until
> quite suddenly
> it takes me in

In such states just to look on a conker is dangerous, sink-
ing into the dark glossy whorls of autumn itself; a chewed

pencil can express infinity in one lead line; a small white feather, drifting on the lawn, opens an unnerving realm of purity and silence. A rose becomes an ocean in which to float or drown; the green verticals of a blade of grass plunge into infinite depths. Suddenly I have seized more than I meant to, more than was wise without grounding or steadying myself; it is safer—even necessary—to scramble back. London buses have a notice on the rear platform that reads, "Stand clear of inward-opening door." Every time I read that, I take it as a barbed rebuke to myself.

> *Stand clear of inward-opening door.*
> Stand very clear. And all obeyed,
> gripping the handrails as the bus
> slewed fast to right and left, bags stayed,
> slipping, but safe. A poet, though,
> stood there, legs loose, a few half-cast
> lines in his pocket, just to feel
> the tall glass crush him, or flash past
> skin-close, allow him through—
> having work to do.

Against the hazards of interior journeys, inspiration seems much easier: a simple openness to whatever comes in the air and touches the heart, or the nape of the neck, with a fresh awareness of life. Some moments swarm with it. I remember one night in Menorca, in a sultry June, when the air seemed full of hints and beckonings, if I could only work them out. Alone in the paved garden, I made the acquaintance of oleanders by moonlight; they glowed with a strange malevolence, a moon-bathed coolness, while their grey leaves hung like flick-knives. I stepped back from going deeper into their shifting, dangerous life, but that meeting told me to observe them, as urgently as words. Mosquitoes whined about me, and I felt one prick minutely on my arm: so delicately aimed, poised, that it would surely sip the merest scruple of my blood. For one beat I was both the insect and myself, victim and perpetrator.

At eight the next morning it was already hot; the sky's faint haziness was only hesitation. The round stones on the patio were warm as bread, the lizards hiding, and tiny movements fretted the lavender, needling me with scent. The oleanders, innocuously pretty, were opening their pink flowers beside the bright-blue pool. Every nuance seemed urgent, important. Anything might move me. I was required to go out into the drama of the garden, even without coffee. I was required to pick up my pen. And then?

> I watch and wait. Day wraps me round
> close as a towel, and I alone
> among all waking things sit still,
> thirst-quieted on the warming stone
>
> that rims the terrace. This is where
> the Breath can find me, as it plays
> regardless in the olive tree,
> riffling it silver. Distant haze
>
> clears from the hills. A feral cat
> troubles the slinking shade. Gauze-thin

intrepid flies alight, explore
my writing-hand that grips the pen,

then lets it slide. Hibiscus flowers
open their mouths along the wall
to suck the air. Some movement clips
the undeserving pool: a fall
of oleander leaves, like gall.

It was a poem only of surface glances, superficial; yet per-
haps enough, in its mere looking, to let my life flow into the
garden and the morning, and that life flood into mine.

I said I was "required" to go outside, but nothing exter-
nal compelled me. The compulsion came from myself. My
presence was somehow both necessary and also natural and
inevitable: like the flowering of the blackthorn, or the silvery
seeding of the even lowlier dwarf thistle, which caught my
eye on the Downs once in the last of the evening light.

Even
the dried-out
thistle-husk,
huddling in summer
cattle dust,
breaks into silk
because
it must

Early morning often seems best for these brushes with
heightened life. An hour after dawn, perhaps, when the world

138

still breathes freshness; or in the hush just before it, when the air is full of the tiny, tentative responses of day-life reassembling. The Kentish word for such a morning is *list*, from "listen"—not the infinitive but the imperative. The atmosphere is so rinsed and scoured that sounds can be caught clearly and from far away, as though that sense has vastly extended itself. This is how such dawns were to me as a child, lying in the high double bed in my aunts' house, under the chilly slipping eiderdown, listening.

> The cockerel stands on his gate in the morning star
> just above Lucking's barn, but a hundred miles
> out in the night, a tremble of light that crows
> silvery, crackling, as worn needles do
> over old tracks; and when the day-bird sings
> every sound follows. Whispering woods that stir
> up on the hill, a voice across five stiles,
> young sparrows rushing down the climbing rose,
> chink of a thrush on snails still dewy-new—
> and on the back lawn sunk in sleeping things
> the almond tree in its Communion dress
> dropping its petals with a chime like glass.

Evening, too, seems good, when shapes lose their definition and distant walkers become cautious, as though the thickening light is harder to wade through; as though they are absorbing into themselves the gilding of the sycamores and the vespers of the birds. Landscapes dissolve, colours are muted; a whirl of dust carries consciousness; each rustle acquires significance that quivers, like a nerve, in my own body.

Slight breeze in ivy
mistaken
for a bird,
a quick thought
flickering along a branch—
half-heard
unsought

But appearances can be deceptive; nothing may be seized that way either. I often find myself trying too hard, as I did on that morning in Menorca: longing for admission to some deeper life, which keeps its distance. On a meditation course in north London our group was sent into the garden to write poems, having supposedly filled ourselves all day with the fire-tinged current of divine breath. We spaced ourselves out self-consciously in the overgrown grass, while a Buddha presided by the wall. Almost every part of that garden is still in my mind, as I mentally raked and plundered it for some doorway to deeper worlds. I found nothing there but small, hard, green pears still on the tree, and brought one back indoors with my blank sheet folded round it.

Conversely in some places words came through, though I hardly knew how or why. I remember a hermit's cave in Sicily, unpretentious, not much visited, but with a strange power to weaken my defences as soon as I pushed through the plastic fronds that screened it. To this odd corner I came several times as though inspiration lived there, like an oracle in an oak grove.

Impossible to settle now.
Urgent to find the spot that will call up

the summoning Breath, the song. I drain my glass,
let the door swing, walk to a jumbled group
of pines and sun-bleached stones. Here, in a cave
moss-cooled by dripping walls, a gentle saint
stayed once to make the air his only food
and the hard sapphire sky his sacrament.
He died, and rather than a splendid shrine
iconed in gold, they put a table here
laid with a check cloth, and a fold-up seat
dusty with age. A brass-chained lamp hangs near,
prompting to prayer. Inside a rusty tin
lie candle-ends, a lighter, and a plate
scattered with coins as votive offering.
I add another. In this emptied state
I'll let the Breath possess me, rhythmic, quiet.

This state of natural patience is perhaps most beautifully
portrayed in a painting of the Annunciation by Antonello da
Messina in Palermo, not far from that hermit's cave. Palermo
is a city full of noise: hooting cars and mopeds, shops crash-
ing their metal blinds, children screaming, brass bands, and
kettledrums for some fiesta or another. But at the very heart
of it, right by a street market, sits the Palazzo Abatellis, now
a museum; and there the young Mary, swathed in blue, looks
up timidly, suddenly understanding. Nothing is obvious. No
one is with her. If a bird has passed, as some painters would
have portrayed the Holy Ghost, it has flown down and away
before she saw it. All she knows is that the pages of her prayer
book are fluttering a little. Another life is passing, a brief
wind through stillness. The Word is staying. Other incidents

are sharper, a summons to action. I am stopped in my tracks, made to turn round, by a sudden rearrangement of elements I had taken for granted.

Often, again, birds are involved.

Snow-light.   Suddenly
Dim in the same   hill-fringing woods
confusion of dawn grey   jigsaw
a seagull   into finches
violently   flying
detaches from the sea

Stout pigeons
gorged on corn-cobs
shock from the field-edge,
wheel into slack clouds
building for rain—
become the clouds
become the rain

Such events, Rilke wrote, had to be noticed. He observed especially how high-gliding birds and topmost branches followed the least direction of the air, adjusting to it, surrendering to it, as though absorbed in a power beyond themselves. They rode on the inbreath. Coleridge, watching too, thought the murmuration-flights of starlings were "without volition." I had seen this in gulls, transformed in their sky-gliding from scavengers to spirits; and in two venerable ash trees near the coast road, where the highest leaf-sprays replied to a summer breeze by glittering, then disappearing. Such sights were often thought-provoking. But Rilke insisted this was not enough.

> There are only two great and related movements: the wingbeat of a high bird and the swaying of treetops. These two movements are intended to teach our souls how to live.

For some, compulsive movement seems the best way to be inspired. Aubrey noted that Francis Bacon, when it rained, "[would] take his Coach (open) to receive the benefit of Irrigation, which he was wont to say was very wholsome because of the Nitre in the Aire and the *Universall Spirit of the World*." Around the same time the poet Matsuo Bashō travelled up and down Japan on foot, with wide-brimmed hat and unfurled umbrella, visiting shrines and beauty spots where others had been moved to write. He received much "benefit of Irrigation"; it seemed to rain almost all the time. The ways were arduous, along lonely paths and across high mountains often lost in mist; he was glad to have tied a new strap on his hat and to have rubbed dried leaves on his legs to strengthen them. Various old bodily complaints flared up too, to vex him. But that "wind-swept spirit," that "fluttering drapery" within him that made him write poetry, meant that he could no longer stay idle at home. "The gods," he wrote, "seemed to have possessed my soul and turned it inside out." In the same way, any ordinary Lakeland day of fine rain, fleeting sun, damp cold, would see Wordsworth high on the fells, walking and reciting in the element from which, he knew, poetry would spring. Neighbours recalled him humming and hawing his lines along the roads, testing the song. Failing the fells he would pace back and forth, back and forth, in the woods and lanes near Grasmere, or simply in the garden-orchard, his sister Dorothy on his arm, as if he had to replicate that ceaseless inward rolling of life.

Then, or earlier, a thought would strike and spark; Dorothy reported that William "kindled" with them. The sight of an abandoned sheepfold by Greenhead Ghyll, with its jumbled unhewn stones, put him in mind of the vigorous old shepherd who had often sat there alone, unlabouring now, thinking of his wastrel son; the daffodils beside Ullswater drew him, too, lanky and clumsy, into the dance of stars and constellations; a wild pansy slipped him, as the tiny flower in the wall had slipped Tennyson, to the edge of imponderable emotion. In Bashō's case, inspiration came from deep-pink bush clover tumbled in wave-foam, exchanging elements and colours, or the white hair of an aged friend echoed in a flowering plum tree, one life in another. Like all great poets, he knew words came of their own accord "when you and the object have become one; when you have plunged deep enough into the object to see something like a hidden glimmering there."

Both he and Wordsworth had fixed their thoughts as a light run of sound or rhyme while walking, holding it close, as a bush-clover bloom might be carried in a pocket; or, as Dorothy hinted, as a precious flame might be guarded in the hand. Back in the study, though, or at the inn, pen and ink had to be prepared, and the thought given physical form. It could become the work of hours, days, weeks, to capture what had struck in a moment. Both men struggled mightily with this. Dorothy described Wordsworth's despondency, nervousness, and "bad spirits" as he wrestled his insights—and hers—into poetry on a page. Bashō, delighted by the exquisite lines and colours of the windblown pines of Matsushima, simply decided that his pen was not up to the task. He had nothing to add to the trees. His haikus, delicate as a hair suspended on a leaf, could fix the freshness of aromatic mugwort released by soft spring rain, the keenness of an arrow in the cry of a bird, a mountain's loneliness in the bent back of a farmer digging potatoes. But sometimes even haikus seemed too clumsy. Like an intermittent wind or unsustainable fire, that moment of heightened life faded and disappeared.

Perhaps it lay as much in what was not written down. Motion and spirit also lived in the space where the pen did not trespass, or where the artist—having gently flicked grey shadow-wash onto a sketch of bamboo—lifted his brush from the paper. That silent reservation declared that the artist could not finish the work himself. It had to be left open, as the young man I met under the chestnut tree had to leave unrecorded the life within the leaves.

Rumi explained this reticence exactly.

Touch the cloth of the robe,
but do not pull it towards you.
                    Presence plays with form,
fleeing and hiding as the sky does in water,
now in one place, now nowhere.

These poems are elusive
because the presence is . . .
What you thought to draw lifts off the paper,
as what you love slips from your heart.

He concluded, more than once, "Let that [invisible] musician finish this poem." But how would he finish it? Venturing into a village street after a sudden spring shower, I realised again that there was no knowing.

On least-lying
water after rain
a brief wind sows through
patterns of its own,
geometries of disquiet,
alternatives

Blown almond petals
disarranged
as I suppose
fall into swirls, ellipses
on the tarmac,
configurations
perfect as a rose

Rumi, watching puddles, too, and the leaf-litter that floated on them, concluded that the wind was only part of the picture. Those insubstantial things, those straws, were "following the love they have been given."

On a London bus once a thistledown drifted lightly

among the passengers, touching a cheek here and an arm there, brushing the windows like a spectral moth. Where it did not go seemed as deliberate as where it did, between the dreaming souls. After five stops or so (ignoring several chances before), it left by the usual doors. Not many noticed it. Those who did mostly disregarded it. But a few passengers it seemed to soothe and mesmerise, spinning invisible webs among them like the threads that bind up wounds. No one thought to catch it; left alone, it completed its purpose, whatever that was. Such delicate rearranging could also be done to me.

> Not to be feared perhaps
> that rhythmic
> shivering through the blood—
> new delicacy of skin
> steadily made porous,
> paper   To write
>   or to be written on

One afternoon in late summer, a red balloon blew across the Downland field where I was walking. I had no idea how it came there. No house was close, no shouting child, no brouhaha of a party. The wide green hills were empty, though invaded now by a fragile globe as shocking and live as blood.

The balloon had been inflated recently. It was full, tight, bouncing with energy, trailing a long string that I tried to catch, but it flicked away too fast. As if it knew my path, it bounded just ahead of me, not so much a companion as a challenge and a tease. I followed after, running to keep up with this messenger which, suddenly, I couldn't bear to lose.

It surely could not live long. The summer breeze, mild but strong, blew it west towards a barbed-wire fence. Yet after feinting in the face of it, grazing the very barbs, carrying my fear with it, the balloon soared over in a single glide. Then it sailed on across the broad valley, towards the sea.

The string zigzagged after it, and not simply the string. My afternoon thoughts went too: all the chance metaphors and scraps I had gathered on the long walk from Eastbourne. I had entered for a while the withered sinews of wild clematis cartwheeling over a hedge, and thistles slowly turning to discs of silver; the deception of wild-strawberry leaves, scarlet as the crushed fruit; a hoverfly, clockwork black and yellow, amorously buzzing my watch, and sheep gathering like grey stones in shade. I had jotted odd words in the notebook, held the sparks carefully in my hand, occasionally reviewing them, encouraging them to survive. Now all had been disarranged. Instead, still travelling across the valley, waywardly dipping and slipping, drifting and shining, my life was caught up with this balloon.

> Flat, compressed to dark, the red balloon
> lies packaged tight with others,
> dead to touch;
> separates flaccidly, inflates
> reluctantly, sour rubber
> puckering too much—

> then starts to swell, impulsive, tip and spring
> to readiness, glass-skin
> taut, squeaking dry;
> keen now to test the coiled controlling string
> by which its breath and life are knotted in,
> compelled at last to fly.

The soaring balloon might have been another of Rilke's "great movements," with the topmost branches and the high birds. Breath within and breath beyond had become the same, and that oneness was intoxicating. I could compare it then only to walking in strong wind, leaning into it or leaning on it, spreading arms to embrace it, as if it could invade my body and transform thought, breaking all resistance down.

The crows I had seen above the Lewes road, fluttering and somersaulting like blown-away bags, naturally grasped it. Wordsworth longed, when skating, to give his body to the wind. Children, knowing boundlessness, readily play that game. In 1798 Coleridge, walking in the Quantocks, came upon two toddlers rejoicing in the gale:

> hair floating, tossing, a miniature of the agitated Trees, below which they play'd—the elder whirling for joy, the one in petticoats, a fat Baby, eddying half willingly, half by the force of the Gust—driven backward, struggling forward—both drunk with the pleasure, both shouting their hymn of Joy.

There is danger in this too. On some walks I have been harried by the wind until I seem transparent as film and cannot feel the clothes on my back. I am just another obstacle for the gale to get past, or over, or through, insignificant as grass or litter lying in the road; another object for the wind to impose its patterns on.

Across
the green-gold
barley
slash
a hundred
silver
scythes

Rushing on past
the wind of countless voices
is a howl in the thorn,
a tug in the fleece,
a dog
panting on the path,
a horse
blustering in the copse,
the kick
of a child still womb-bound,
and a boy
testing his echo
in the last
valley
left

In permanent gale
thundering
against my eyelids
one gust

> one instant
> pulls back,
> weighs up its prey—
> my hand
> extended to it
> is knocked away

Then, very occasionally, something different happens. On one holiday in Portugal, sitting outside a sunshine-yellow café with my friends, I was so elated by a vast scallop shell of clouds in the sky that I found myself clinging to my yellow chair and struggling, fighting, not to be swept away. The sensation was the same as when I try to enter the life of flowers or stones: vertigo, expanded being, and near-irresistible attraction. Yet the day was completely windless; we would have gone sailing otherwise. The turmoil was within me, not without, and I wrestled with it smiling and drinking, ostensibly calm, while my friends felt nothing. At one point, past the yellow blind, I sensed the whole sky opening to pull me through, not violently but almost tenderly, as if reclaiming me. I half wanted to resist it and half longed, like Coleridge's children and Rilke's high birds, to surrender and "learn how to live."

The only thing comparable, I thought later, was inexpressible mutual love.

Tim Samaras was in love with storms. He was a weather researcher in Oklahoma: not one of the gawping thousands whose cars clogged the state's roads in tornado season, but an engineer who had made his own instruments and probes to measure the temperature, static pressure, and humidity of storms and find out what went on inside them. Antennae perched like whirligigs on the top of his car could detect the speed of higher winds. Ground-level ones he would estimate by watching dry sticks or maple leaves that blew in front of him, observing as keenly, and with a sense of intrinsic involvement, as a poet would. He also carried Doppler radar, and an extra-high-speed camera expressly to catch lightning. The orange probes were his trademark, set in the storm's path almost as part of the whole performance.

Yet this was not entirely a scientific enterprise. He had fallen for storms at the age of six, watching with amazement the lowering skies and the tumbling house in *The Wizard of Oz*. That twister was a black beast rampaging over the plain, plucking up small trees and sending the horse running out of the stable, but it was also beautiful. The word often sprang to his lips when he talked about tornadoes: beauty in the towering, narrowing funnel, the continuous roaring, the smell of grass fresh-scythed by the wind and earth torn open by it.

In his longing to commune with the wind and understand it, he often got too close. Near Manchester, South Dakota, he encountered a tornado (measuring EF4 on the Enhanced Fujita scale) strong enough to rip telephone poles out of the ground and absorb them into itself. In the eighty-two seconds before the storm reached him, he just had time to position his probes on the road; they registered the steepest fall in atmospheric pressure ever recorded, one hundred millibars in less than a minute, as the twister passed over. On one clip from his video camera, his son Paul could be heard shouting that they didn't have time, they didn't have time, *seriously*.

Samaras took some care, staying in his car with seatbelt fastened when he was caught up in that "bear's cage" of whipping wind wrapped in rain. Yet he was also in love, and like a boy would run irrepressibly to any window when it rattled. On May 31, 2013, he was killed chasing an EF5 at El Reno, which suddenly whirled round from east to north and sent his car tumbling for half a mile. His orange probes, however, kept recording, as though at another level he still observed the storm.

Coleridge in 1806, unhappily in love, despairing that his life would ever add up to much, wrote of being "whirled about without a center—as in a nightmair—no gravity—a vortex without a center." Yet he was also well aware of a centre, in his guttering tallow candle and in himself, where a steadier fire seemed to burn. He was both the wind and the power that could tame it, strongly, analytically, within himself: both the draught-torn flame and the still, focused core.

One stormy winter night, watching from my Brighton windows, I saw a similar drama going on.

> In weltering
> dark-wrecked
> cities of waves
> one fishing boat
> gleams out
> from time to time,

not tossed, lost
as random sparks may be
but in some deeper gulf
fixed,
maybe,
calm,
maybe
shining

3. Indwelling

THE STRONGEST POWER OF NATURE I HAVE KNOWN is not wind or storm, but birth. No primer prepared me for the violence of a life-force beyond my control. All those chapters on yogic posture, soothing oils, and aroma-balm went out of the window; the Mozart tapes I had brought with me, to welcome the new arrival gently into the world, were forgotten and also lost. Instead, what happened was chaos. My husband's keenest memory of it, when he had steeled himself to stay, was the midwife gesticulating wildly at the foot of the bed, shouting, "What I do now?" As births go, though, it was perfectly normal: just life at its most commanding and most implacable.

And my most vivid recollection was of stillness. Not of labour, a dim-lit turbulence of pain eclipsed immediately by the astonishment of my son at my breast, but of standing beforehand in the white-tiled hospital shower. As I watched the tepid water flowing over my enormous belly, knotted with thick veins and shining streams, I realised, with total calm, that I was ready. I was part of a greater power; I could face anything that happened. I was steady and practical, like the young woman I had seen on the beach in Brighton one morning, caught in the early haze.

> Ankle-deep
> in blue infinity
> > the swimmer halts—
> > adjusts
> > her slim black
> > shoulder-strap

I was involved, too, in something illimitably far beyond myself; an enterprise that depended on me, naked, ridiculous and soapy as I was, and of which even the stars were somehow curiously aware. I had a feeling of consequence, even importance, in the great scheme of things: the same feeling I had had when I was myself a child.

> So slightly swinging
> on the long low
> lateral
> of the ash
> I move
> the whole
> green
> cosmos
> of the tree

My firstborn was about to appear. I had never asked, but sensed that he was male; and I had already dreamed of him, not as a baby but as a dark-haired young man. He was leaving a house in the hills, locking the door and setting out, in a tall black hat and floating black coat. An antique bicycle leaned beside the wall, but he did not mount it; instead he walked, wheeling the bike, down the long steep road towards the world.

I generally read nothing into dreams. They seem to point to neither future nor past, just to slightly detached adventures in the present. The landscapes I vaguely recognise; some-one in the ghost-crowd that mills about will tell me this is Chichester or Bulgaria, and I, looking around me, will know that to be true. For a while I dreamed so repeatedly of a cer-tain path between two places, passing at one stage through a wood and at another through a house—all quite unknown in my daytime life—that I could take shortcuts in it without the usual dream deviation. At another frequent dream-place, a suburban north London street backed by great chalk hills, I said to myself: "So this is where those hills *really* are, that I keep seeing in dreams."

I concluded then that this was another world opening out of my life; or perhaps another life, out of the world. As with those hills, dreams often correct other dreams, insisting that they are showing me what is real. This is a life where I can cry, feel annoyed, be scared, make love, but all those things can probably be explained by the activity of the still-awake brain. It is odder (given that both speech and hearing are muffled in my dreams) that I can chew and taste the food I'm given at extravagant buffets, drive a car with proper attention, and feel a stone balustrade (though, on touching, it may crumble into sand). It is odder still that I can remember, from decades ago, walking up my great-aunts' lane, kicking pinecones from the rough grass, to stand at a gate and see old Mrs. Fisher sitting peacefully amid the ruins of her house. Her hair was in a neat grey bun, as always, and she wore her usual flowered apron; she smiled sweetly and offered me biscuits. In fact she no longer lived there, because she had been bombed out a decade before I was born. In reality (as far as I can trust it) I never met her, or even saw her in a photograph. But the scene was so vivid that I believed for years, indeed knew, that it had happened in full consciousness. I had felt the pinecones rolling underfoot; I had recognised her, regretted refusing her biscuits, and went on adding those details, and the bombed house, to my actual remembrances of life. In effect, I had lived another past. Now, when I review my early memories, I wonder how easily I can unravel them from dreams.

Perhaps a neurologist could explain. There is generally a haziness and lightness to the body in dreams, a sense of floating rather than being, in the earthly sense. These waking dreams, as I think of them, are quite different. I am physically, heavily, consciously present; I know I have been bodily transplanted, or transported, somewhere else. Here and there. In another such dream—which I did not think a dream at the time—I found myself in the sitting room of my childhood suburban house, standing by the window, watching thin snow begin to fall on the empty street and the darkened greengrocer's opposite. Everything was exact, down to the peculiar, variegated pattern on the carpet, which I had not remembered until then. I presumed that, to anyone entering the room, I would have been a ghost. In another instance I was in a battered leather armchair in the crown of a tree, suddenly there without climbing, gripping the worn arms as the tree swayed, as if dropped by a bird. Such a realisation is astounding, frightening and, at the same time, intensely delicate. I know it cannot possibly last long, it is too strange; I am trespassing, and sense strongly that I should not be there. I feel desperate to prolong it in order to fathom it, but have no idea how. I am two people in two lives—actor and sleeper—with no idea which life is real; unless, by some unnerving miracle, both are.

In one such dream I found myself lying on a clifftop, looking down on a bright-blue bay fringed with misty mountains and faint spired castles, like a scene from a book of hours. In my longing to stay, or at least to remember, I tore up some of the wiry grass and put it in my jacket pocket. I was sure at the time I would find it the next day; everything was so real, it could not possibly be otherwise. But the next day there was nothing there. I'm tempted to add "of course," but it was much less certain than that. In fact I was almost too afraid to check: afraid it might indeed be there, and what that would mean if it was.

Those rare experiences are by far the oddest dreams. Yet the people in that world also intrigue me. One or two friends, relations, or colleagues may well appear and even star, but everyone else is a stranger. At least, a stranger in my waking world; but in dreams I know their whole history, their importance, and their place in my life, as they know mine in theirs. The more such known-but-unknown characters bustle through a scene, the more I puzzle, when I wake up, over where they can have come from. I presume I have remembered those faces from a mere glance, on-screen, in a newspaper, or in the supermarket queue, and recreated them whole and entire to populate another world. But that seems too impressive and strange a skill. Are they, as some psychiatrists think, projected aspects of myself? If they are, does that also apply to the world I doggedly think of as real?

In the case of my unborn son, his face glimpsed for mere seconds, I knew he was not from my past. In fact he was from my future, and his face became my son's in his twenties. His presence in the dream was not part of any larger drama—this was an episode by itself, simply, it seemed, to show that he was coming. Yet I knew both who he was and what he was doing, as in dreams we firmly know the most improbable things. He was coming to inhabit the new body, colouring it with memories and affinities from elsewhere, overlaying his past and even his future on the present. The life I was about to welcome was, in a sense, brand-new, and in a sense outside all time. This traveller through other worlds was on his way to mine.

That conclusion was startling, but in the hospital it seemed confirmed. I found myself holding close, and listening for, both new life and old life.

> I knew your squalling on the labour ward,
> knew it as mine, or of me, even in
> a dozen nursery cries. I stood absurd
>
> in flowery folds of nightgown, ravening
> for eggs and bacon, sulking to make do
> with white bread and stewed tea, still havering
>
> and somehow undelivered, slippering through
> more urgent corridors. Again there came
> those tiny gasping cries for milk, as though

it might be air, or both perhaps the same
sustenance, thin as water, cloudy-white
as winter's mist along the window frame.
You hungered long before you had a name.

Those cries came from the baby room then, down past
the clanking trolleys and the sterile swinging doors; but I felt
they rang from much further away. From the Downs, with
their processions of ghosts, and from the past: elemental
cries, like the gibber of a bird or the mewing of a kitten, or
the insistent pant of the wind.

These are the echoes, far-off incantations
of those who went before us, up this track,
over this Down. Harsh hospital vibrations

surround you now, but faint thrums winding back
record a girl who walks in cowhide shoes
fastened with gorse-darts, leading by the hand

a low-browed child; or men with lambs out loose
striding in hobnails, wind-whipped dogs at knee,
eyes pale as chalk. Their shouts have gone, diffuse

threads in the breeze, but deep and rhythmically
their tread goes on with ours. Grass under feet
digs down, springs up; wands from the hazel tree

twist out pure water; and some silver-bead
sense of those souls remains, a residue

glinting on clover, sparkling on green wheat—
studding as fresh bud or as ancient seed.

At each cry my breasts tightened and sticky milk ran down my skin, which I would lamely try to hide or laugh at. But that instant physical connection was also disturbing: the same life deeply joining us, who had never wittingly known each other before. Looking into my son's eyes, a few hours after giving birth to him, I found myself staring into a darkness that seemed infinite, the depth of the universe, ancient and wise. And yet just arrived, here, mine.

So now you sleep, tired new-born mariner.
Sleep of furled sheets and twisting of oiled jute
around the capstan; sleep of dulcimer

beneath my fingers, and the soft-mouthed flute
of my plugged nipple, muffling out the sea
and symphony of stars. Held to your route

by rigid bed-rails, you sleep fitfully,
moment by moment jerking, arms flung wide
into the universe where you sailed free

only to land here. Through that first full night
we struggled, you and I, the Mogadon
not working, and the air thick with your slight

fussed whimpering, like words. What's done is done.
I saw your day-old fresh-bewildered face

when you awoke; all you had known was gone.
You were a blank leaf to be written on.

I did not imagine those night sounds; my son seemed to be arguing with himself, justifying himself, reconciling himself to where he was, as any adult might. At that point, I even felt guilty for my part in what had happened to him.

> Your crib is wickerwork.
> How fashionable it seems:
> sprigged cambric at the sides,
> a vehicle of dreams,
>
> flat-bottomed, safe. Inside,
> the birth-card that I've drawn,
> a rose and butterfly
> crayoned blue, wrapped neat in lawn
>
> I hemmed for you, slant stitch
> by stitch embodying you,
> holding your weight. Perhaps
> I sewed your prison too,
> pulling the tight thread through.

I was thinking of lines I had loved and instinctively believed for years, those of Wordsworth's great "Immortality Ode":

> Our birth is but a sleep and a forgetting;
> The Soul that rises with us, our life's Star,

Hath had elsewhere its setting,
And cometh from afar . . .

But I may have exaggerated such resistance in my son's case. There may well have been no inherent opposition, just one infant life in which spirit and material worked in concert from the outset. Perhaps that blank leaf was not a loss or an absence, but the necessary first condition: eternal soul and temporary, perishable body both flung into newness, each essential to the other, compelled together to rediscover and recreate the world.

Enough of all this dualism, even if
some feel it's true; let sackcloth saints insist
the body is an ass hung down with firewood,
feed-bags, corncobs, knives and forks,
obstructive appetites—

Perhaps instead they dance a pasodoble,
body and soul in quick-step clenched embrace
with forty couples in a Spanish square,
filling the band-space, strutting, swivelling necks
under the half-moon lights—

Or else the body's docile, shouldering
the great wood platform of carnation-blood
and *pasos* of the saints, when it is asked;
while soul, in white-wool robes, clacks castanets
to mark each ease-down and phone-scan relax—
each inbreath, straightening backs.

In my Catholic childhood I had seen soul as another part of the body, like my lungs or my liver. It lay somewhere near my heart, kept like the Eucharist in a sort of satin-lined tabernacle into which the Devil could never thrust his rough red hand as our wheezing old priest thrust his. There it shone, as if it was the Host itself. When I misbehaved, it acquired grey stains; but I could easily clean it again. When I committed grievous sins, stealing my brother's sweets or slipping a little German dictionary into my pocket in a bookshop, it grew sooty, like an occluded moon. I had hurt soul then, and my business was to make it shine as brightly as before.

Yet my soul was not my life. It seemed to me a fragile thing, shrinking and silken, shivering in strange interior draughts, although it was meant never to go out. For whatever reason—for the ways of childhood are often strange—I associated it with the thin, half-withered rose that grew in our suburban garden. They were connected by that same feeling of frailty, sadness, and otherworldliness, as though they were too good to stay long.

> Dear rose, pale-fevered as a dying saint
> beside the creosote fence, I gently hold
> my face to yours. Your perfume lies so faint,
> so weakly held, each petal ivory-cold,
> blots on your leaves. They mean to cut you down
> one year—they always say so—but you stay,
> your heart choked up with stamens rusty-brown

as crumpled wire. "Still with us, then!" they say.
And yet already you're so far away.

That tenderness lasted years, far longer than the rose itself. I forgot it later. But I am still moved by the golden core of a wild rose, the hub of a perfect fivefold geometry, and by the diffidence of the tiny creatures that visit it, thunder-bug or wood wasp, pausing in their woodland dustiness as though they are approaching a shrine. Even the earliest buds of the wild rose seem to anticipate holiness, their outer petals lifting like tissue or like veils. In my own holy moods—which I enjoyed with the fresh-washed intensity of any naughty child—I knew my soul and I were companions in love, and sat with it somewhere near the portico of heaven.

For this, I was sure, was where soul owed its loyalty. Heaven, soul, and God were all in contact with each other, like an array of lights along a road. Soul did not affect—let alone direct—the workings of my body, but spied on them like another eye. It was not myself, but a watcher of myself. I often felt that it did not understand the world, or quite understand me, and that I should explain.

Other ideas of the soul gradually intruded. Plato's soul, an angel-creature whose feathers fell away on immersion in Earth-life, and the homunculus medieval people imagined the naked miniature of the self found hiding in the birth-bed curtains or rising from the mouth at death, journeying to repentance. Through these I formed an idea of the learning, suffering soul, adapting to the capacity of one particular body at one particular time: no longer the static, separate Host but divinity discovering, through hands, feet, eyes, and brain, the struggles and joys of human life. I also began to see the soul less as Wordsworth's star, with its curious passivity, than as the body's life and self-consciousness. And I recognised how, through the stages of life, that consciousness changed.

It was sometimes shocking. Just before my fifteenth birthday I saw my first *Hamlet*; immediately afterwards I started wearing different clothes, identified with different literary characters, and found my writing sloping to the right, while my politics sloped left. At times my inner life altered so abruptly that I no longer recognised the thoughts I had recorded only a few years before. I threw them out, the diaries and the small blue duplicate books, burying them deep in the recycling, embarrassed even by the neat, obsessive handwriting. To reject them, I knew, was to betray or deny someone I had been. But I was not that person anymore, and I could not bear to leave history a portrait that was no longer true.

Some aspects of soul, however, were unvarying. The core of this life force stayed where I had imagined it in childhood, somewhere near my heart, twinned with it possibly, body and soul together. When love or music moved me, both heart and soul expanded with pain and sweetness. And there was always, as I saw it, a brightness there: a residual brightness and the silence of deep space to which, somehow, it also belonged. Keats spoke of his soul as a "hushed casket." Rumi wrote of "a secret heart-house" where it lay: a deep, silent mirror in which a flame burned and moved rhythmically to the music of the heavenly flute player, reflected and returned. In the Hindu Upanishads, equally, the soul was a flame living in "the secret place of the heart." Insofar as mystics pictured it within the body, it was always in the form of fire: the heat of life and its flaring, serpentine energy, emerging out of infinite dark.

The tendencies of my soul were also strangely unchanging. Much as I wanted to suppress my past self, many aspects remained: my constant urge to write, my obsession with tidiness and tiny things, my yearning to find landscapes known only from picture books, my habit of falling rapturously in love with people who were unattainable. I recognised myself in "my blue," that old longing, whenever it ambushed me. It was as if, like Cedric Robinson, I felt my ashplant hit bedrock under the shifting sands—or as if, like Claudio Abbado, I heard beneath the whirling snow the note of silence itself.

I was clearly wrong, then, to have thought soul weak or delicate. The reverse was true. It was often stubborn and insistent. In the presence of beauty or high purpose it regained its shining feathers, as Plato said, and soared in its proper element again. At times I could feel that movement, and its strength was my strength. Tripping over a stone once, certain to fall, I felt the centering force of soul seize and reset me with a curious, determined slowness. Cliff-bound on another day, unable to move up or down the slipping, near-vertical chalk, I felt it push me up beyond any power I could muster myself. In the museum at Heraklion in Crete soul is summed up in a small Minoan bronze of a bull-leaper, one of those ecstatic young men who would run towards a bull and dive for the back or the horns. The bronze shows the leaper in that moment of triumph: the decision taken, the chest thrown out, the lithe body, like the soul, flying.

On a wave invisible, a wave of air,
flinging up arms, his body sleek,
poised, weight-defying, all at once
he leaps at the hard horns levelled to rip him raw;
grasps, vaults, somersaults, while just below
rushes the huge humped black and thundering surge
sent to destroy him. Thus we see fate
making straight for us, time or death towering
and booming, but look! we flip over
loosely, lightly, the looming head, and are left—
cradled in feathering foam, white flowers.

That statue proclaimed that when humans surrender to soul-power, then they are gods.

Yet dependence on soul may be far more everyday than that. It may be that in every least action, like the raising of an arm or the cradling of a head, we employ a greater power. This is the teaching of the Hindu mystics. That "god who is in the heart" breathes in and breathes out, rhythmically ruling all the body's actions through millions of tiny channels—nerves, we might say—flowing with the flame of life. The Kena Upanishad explains this multiplicity in a few understated lines.

What cannot be spoken with words, but that whereby
    words are spoken—know that alone to be Brahman,
    Spirit . . .
What cannot be thought with the mind, but that whereby
    the mind can think—know that alone to be Brahman,
    Spirit . . .

What cannot be seen with the eye, but that whereby the eye
    can see—know that alone to be Brahman,
    Spirit . . .
What cannot be indrawn with breath, but that by which
    breath is indrawn—know that alone to be Brahman,
    Spirit, and not what people here adore.

According to the Vedas, and not only to them, the bound-less and timeless life of the universe is in ourselves, as ourselves. The moment it enters is disputed, whether at birth, quicken-ing, or conception; at first it may be the life of a seed, a rooting plant, a forming human without thought. But when a body is complete, ready for the first breath and the first cry, soul-life is there in fullness; it cannot be kept out. It is all life, as far as we can handle it; it is all one. In St. John's gospel, Jesus makes the point: "He who abides in Me, and I in him, brings forth much fruit; for without Me you can do nothing." Even stern St. Paul in 1 Corinthians admits it: "There are diversities of operations, but it is the same God which worketh all in all."

The Kaushitaki Upanishad perhaps puts it best:

    The breath of life is one;
    When we speak, life speaks.
    When we see, life sees.
    When we hear, life hears.
    When we think, life thinks.
    When we breathe, life breathes.

Rumi, as ever, summed up in a line: "I looked for myself, and found only God."

The idea is almost too hard to grasp. If touched for a moment it disappears, like a dazzle of light on water. But it seems to me too glorious and too challenging simply to brush aside. Dante began to sense it when, struggling through the hills of hell, he found himself possessed of more breath and power than he had known he had. Aristotle taught that each person and thing had a purpose, a *telos*, that went beyond themselves. And the everyday expression of that extraordinary indwelling is the *namaste*, the bow with hands joined, which in Covid times replaced most other signs of affection and respect: "The god in me salutes the god in you."

Whenever I write of someone else, I try to be alert to this: to catch that universal essence, that true fire, in every life. It is not a religious principle, unless my subjects make it so. I see it as scientific as much as spiritual. The evidence of soul is often flickering or has been ripped out, suppressed, as I suppressed mine. It tends to gleam more strongly in childhood or old age than in the busy, distracted middle decades of a career. And though it dwells in both the good and the bad, in some the sense of soul-power burns so steadily that the world around is changed.

One of these beings was Brother Roger, the tiny, luminous founder of the Taizé religious community, who decided to stay in the deep stillness of the village that he had cycled into in 1940, in the midst of war elsewhere. Around one hundred people lived there, in the woods and rugged valleys of *la France profonde*. A few sandstone houses, some empty, made up the place. The road was unsurfaced, and there was no telephone; the world did not come through here. He might have gone on, but an old woman pressed him to remain. "We are lonely," she told him.

As soon as I mentally entered Taizé with Roger Schütz, as he was then, I felt inclined to stay myself. I trod quietly. My writing slowed down as I watched him dismount and walk, talk to the old woman, shed the weight of his bags. Already running through my mind was one of the chants that had come from Taizé into my own church, hundreds of miles away: Christ's instruction to his apostles as he entered the garden of Gethsemane.

> Stay with me
> remain here with me,
> watch and pray

This lost corner had not always been so silent. Ten minutes away lay the ruins of the great Benedictine abbey of Cluny, which had once been full of melody and chant sung to the glory of God. Taizé, on that same "inspired hill," still echoed with what Shelley called "the memory of music fled." It was the ideal place for Brother Roger, as he soon became, to found an order whose ritual was based on the principles of music and silence. As he built his church there, out of the grey local stone, he chanted Divine Office in the woods, restoring sacred music to them. Once his church was complete, he filled it with mantras that moved beneath the prayers and became, for him, his all-sustaining "pillar of fire." He died in that communion with Life, his throat cut by a disturbed woman in the place he had made holy again. Thousands continue to visit it, and millions to chant his songs.

I think also of Baba Amte, a rich Kolkata lawyer who touched, by mistake, the rotting body of a leper in the gutter. The face and hands had already gone, and maggots crawled in livid flesh; the man was dying. At first, Amte ran away. But he overcame his horror to lift the leper up, learn his name—Tulshiram—take him home, and nurse him from oblivion back to life. From then on, he did not bother with his membership of the tennis club.

His ashram, founded in 1949 on barren, rocky land full of snakes, was specifically for lepers and the handicapped, who built and tilled it from scratch with half a dozen tools and their stumps of hands. It was called Anandwan, "the grove of joy." Here they transformed the apparently useless land with plots of millet, grains, and fruit, and rebuilt their own world of helpless railway station begging into a town of three thousand people, with colleges, two hospitals, workshops, and an orchestra. Not by tears, but by sweat, Amte wrote once, and noted how similar those two things were. In his later years, almost immobile and cot-bound from degeneration of the spine, he went to live by the Narmada River to prevent a huge dam from being built there. He raised another ashram beside it on the stony, empty ground. Each day, until he grew too frail and the muddy banks too hazardous, he would be taken to the river to watch it flow; for to him, though he was not religious, the Narmada was a goddess whose beauty should be decorated only with micro-dams on a human scale. Nor should it carry his ashes away, for they should stay in the earth, recreating it from within.

Both those men were evidently saints. Aretha Franklin seemed at first entirely different. Her songs were raunchy and angry, berating the latest useless man as a no-good heart-breaker, a liar, and a cheat. Men in general didn't begin to give her what she wanted, that bit of respect when she came home. She demanded respect from managers too: to be called Ms. Franklin, to be spared air-conditioning, and to be paid in cash. Big-shot would-be producers in New York were told, frankly, "I want hits."

Yet the Queen of Soul also had another side. When in the course of a concert she shrugged her strong shoulders out of some satiny dress or flung away her long fur coat to sing "You Make Me Feel Like a Natural Woman," she wasn't addressing any sexy superlative lover, whatever the press thought. What looked like a concert platform or a stadium stage had become the New Bethel Baptist Church in Detroit, where she had sung as a child. Her father was pastor there, so it was expected, but she was painfully shy, hiding behind both the piano and the firm comforting words of "Jesus Be a Fence Around Me." That trusting habit stayed. Wherever she was, she could build her own church. Her life was tough, with a mother who walked out when she was six, two babies by different men before she was fifteen, and a slick pimp of a manager-husband who beat her. But she sang to the one who knew her best, saw the bruises she covered up, and did not walk out on her. Music took her to where he was, and he was always there, claiming her from the Lost and Found, taking her hand to lead her through: Almighty Fire, Almighty Love.

Yet the subject who seemed to come closest to pure soul was none of these. He was a clown. His life was lived entirely in reverie or imagination, that state in which—as Shelley, and others long before him, liked to say—poets and God are cocreators of the world. He was no saint or angel, but a simple figure struggling, like all others, with human existence: alternately funny and unsettling, innocent and challenging, foolish and good. To some people, he might have been a Holy Fool.

His name was Bip. In September 2007 it was his alter ego, the mime artist Marcel Marceau, who had died. But it was Bip whose disappearance was mourned, celebrated, and remembered. Bip, to Marceau, was his own soul, discovering everything anew, yet "alone in a fragile world filled with injustice and beauty." This was how I recorded him:

When the spotlight finally faded on Bip, leaving not even a hand or a flower illuminated, it caused only a sigh of surprise. Bip had tried many times to put an end to himself. He would cut his wrists with a blade, nicking and wincing away from it, in case his copious blood gushed over his pure-white sailor's trousers. He would shake out into his palm a handful of pills, open his wide red mouth and fail to swallow them. Stepping on a chair that wobbled under him, he would knot a noose round his scrawny neck, test it, yank it, gyrate his head like a pigeon, and step out into the void. Nothing worked. He went on living.

His wish to die was also not surprising. Often he was kept, crouching or standing, in an invisible cage on the empty stage. One by one he ran his hands along the bars until, with all his strength, he pushed two apart and jumped nimbly out; but then, right ahead of him, behind him, all around him, he found his palms flattening against a wall of glass. Each cage was contained in another. His hands often became birds, flickering and fluttering out of his sleeves, and he made them fly swiftly from their prisons, laughing as they flew. But around him the bars soon closed tightly again.

He dreamed; but his dreams were rarely successful. He hunted butterflies with a darting net, only—accidentally—to break their wings. He plucked flowers, then picked their petals out admiringly and was surprised they died. When he tried to tame lions, they ate him, scorning the thin hoop that he flourished in their direction. He walked against wind and made no progress. His black-ringed eyes and black-lined eyebrows registered sadness, wonder, perplexity, and terror. But he did not know what malevolence was.

To the naked eye, Bip had only the clothes he stood up in: trousers, jacket, soft ballet shoes, striped jersey, and a crumpled opera-hat topped with a red flower. His lean limbs and white face were his only language. The spotlight played on him, and nothing else.

Yet the silence around him was filled with the world he created: chairs, tables, animals, trunks, and escalators. It swarmed with lounging waiters, officious policemen, dog-walkers pulled to right and left, old ladies knitting. Railway trains roared through, and Bip, bounding and swaying in his seat, struggled to keep his suitcase from falling out of the rack. The sea flooded in, bringing a ship that could take him to America, Japan, or Australia, and he staggered manfully up and down the pitching deck.

He never spoke. His alter ego, Marceau, had lost his father in Auschwitz, and Bip's silence was a tribute to all who had been silenced in the camps. In one of his acts, "Bip Remembers," the sad-faced clown relived in mime the horrors of war and stressed the necessity of love. In another, his hands became good and evil: evil, clenched, and jerky; good, flowing, and emollient, with good marginally winning.

His alter ego sometimes spoke for him, in Bip's clothes, to explain him to the crowd: "If I do this, I feel that I am a bird. If I do this, I am a fish. And I feel that, if I do this, it's like a song . . . To mime the wind, one becomes a tempest. Mime expresses . . . the soul's most secret aspiration."

Bip was also, he said, "a hero of our time. His gaze is turned not only towards heaven, but into the hearts of men." Marceau compiled his soul's biography and painted his portrait, colouring him blue, rose, and mauve as he walked through city streets and sailed among the stars. He also wrote a poem for him.

A silent, fragile hand has drawn in space a white flower
    emptied of its blood.
Soon it will open, blossom out. Soon, though faded, bloom
    again.

4. Returning

MOST OF MY OBITUARIES ARE CELEBRATIONS OF life. My subjects, whether famous or unknown, are full of years, and have enhanced the world by their existence. I seldom mention a cause of death; usually the body wore out, that is all. That sojourn is over, the song is sung; the grave is dug and piled with flowers, and spirit passes on.

The process is so universal that it should lighten the thought of death. New grass grows over last year's withered stalks; celandines shine from the leaves that cobweb the floor of the wood; grey-scaled lichen on a dead branch gapes tiny orange trumpets, as nestlings do. Tired, spent forms make way for new ones. Life out of death, as when I came up Friston Hill and passed the sexton coming down, carrying the Passiontide churchyard cross with its sashes of blood-red and white; and we both brushed socially-distantly under the blackthorn that breathed out resurrection.

In another churchyard, in a distant July, my farmer- brother was called in to clear the rampant weeds with his scythe. Not a billhook or a sickle: a proper scythe, with a handle taller than he was and a huge, curved, dark blade. "That devil-thing," his friends called it. Death's implement. To see him with it among the graves was startling at first, even frightening. As he swung it with a proud, straight back, or simply stood with it (strange how a scythe lends elegance to a man), I was aware that the only other figure I had seen with one was a capering skeleton or cloaked in black.

It was fascinating to watch him, as in some film from the sepia past. His blade sliced easily through hawkweed and sow-thistles, but in the lank swathes of grass it soon blunted and jarred. Every ten minutes or so he had to stop, apply a nine-inch whetstone, and hone the blade again. The whetstone hissed, and the scythe itself made a low sighing in the grass. Job's sighs; Henry Purcell's sighs.

> Man that is born of a woman
> Hath but a short time to live
> And is full of misery;
> He cometh up, and is cut down like a flow'r.
> He fleeth as it were a shadow,
> And ne'er continueth . . .
> And ne'er continueth in one stay.

You could say this was a scene of death, but it did not feel like one. The sun was hot, and flies were bothersome. My brother wore a gaudy binding round his hat and a red bandanna dark with sweat and cursed amiably while he worked. The grass that wilted under his blade would spring again, more luxuriant, within a month or so. Life flowed, like a slow breeze, from one pausing-place to the next.

I imagine Johnny Kingdom whistled too. He was a grave-digger, man and boy, in the parish of Bishop's Nympton in Devon. As a child he went along with his father and grand-father to light their night-work with a Tilley lamp, shivering at the ghost stories they told and at the skulls they sometimes thrust up on their forks. Yet he learned to look death square in the eye, holding up its blank sockets beside his own twink-ling smile and his hat stuck with buzzards' and pheasants' feathers. If it was hot going, digging, he would strip off down to his tattoos. As he worked, there was always a robin about; an old cock pheasant, too, who would perch on the grave-edge and sometimes jump in, as if to say, "Where's you to, then?" When Johnny took a break, laying down spade, pick, and shovel, he liked to watch the ivy-clad churchyard walls where blackbirds nested and snails crept to shelter in the heat of the day.

Out on Exmoor, the most beautiful place in the world to him, he had learned how to ease himself closer to crea-tures. He knew how to tickle trout, slowly stroking their cold, smooth bellies and sides before hooking a finger under a gill to pull them in; how to spear salmon with his dung-pick or creep to kill a deer. Poaching had also been his trade. But eventually, rather than snagging or shooting life and hauling the bloodied bodies away in his van, he would aim a camera to catch it in undamaged beauty. Salmon leaping in a dia-mond spray; his favourite red deer emerging through mist from a wooded cleave; uncoiling adders gaping their pink mouths wide enough to swallow him. He built hides, one from a fallen pylon, one with armchairs, from which to film rare birds and badgers unobserved. If death stalked up in a similar way on him, he already had the measure of that. Under the church tower at Bishop's Nympton, where the ground was always hard, he had already dug his own grave, infilling it with soft earth to make a nice, easy job.

Soft earth, soft bed. The presumed repose of the dead is so profound that it makes the blood of the living move more slowly. Almost any ancient churchyard will cast this spell, but for me the deepest peace is found at Painswick, in Gloucestershire. There a small church with a spire nestles among high hills, crowded in with tombs and enormous close-clipped yews that arch above the path. There are said to be ninety-nine of them; the Devil will not allow any more to grow. Under them lie limestone graves in every imaginable shape: headstones, flatstones, table tombs, pepper pots, and pyramids. Many, in this wool-growing region, commemorate the solid clothiers of the town, and they carry all the para-phernalia of memorial: swags, drapes, lyres, scrolls, winged cherubs. Yet time has rubbed the details away. They have melted into the stone, so that what remains is only the edge of a curtain, a suggestion of urns, the part-frame of a harp. Most evocative of all are the cherub faces, pale and vanishing, like little ghosts. All around them romps the grass, full of daisies, forget-me-nots, and speedwell, ideal flowers to grow among the temporarily resting, journeying dead.

In my own local churchyard in East Sussex a large crab-apple tree reigns over the graves. Its blossom is sparse and not remarkable, but the fruit is another story.

Come August it is everywhere, scattered gold, whether or not its abundant life can be any use in ours.

> No takers this year for the apple crop
> so we rake up the hoard beneath the tree
> almost in apology, not wanting
> to throw them on the compost, or to see
>
> the small soft mouse-gnawed fruit left lying there,
> sliming the mower, trodden into grass.
> The pile shines yellow, high, unruly-rich
> as in those August days the harvest was
>
> when pliant branches sank down tenderly
> heavy among the headstones, swelling
> with eagerness to feed, to give.
> Gary on the back wall, ivy-felling,
> whistles Love divine, all loves excelling.

The lushness of graveyards speaks irresistibly of life continuing and returning. In some places it reappears even more visibly and wondrously. In Michoacán, in western Mexico, it is announced by clouds of orange monarch butterflies that fly in to cover the forests. Since they always arrive around November 2, the Day of the Dead, they are taken as the souls of the ancestors and their colour, marigold bright, is that of the flowers that are laid down to cover the graves.

Homero Gómez had been a logger, felling, chaining, and dragging away the oyamel pines that covered the hills above his village. Yet he had never forgotten the day, January 9, 1975, when as a child of four he had first felt the touch of one of the butterflies. It was as big as his hand, bigger, yet soft, and delicate as crêpe paper. This memory eventually caused him to put aside his chainsaw and build a sanctuary for the monarchs among the pines, to which each year they would return to cluster like silken scarves. At the end of each October he would watch for them.

As they arrived he stood among the hectic swarms, a burly moustachioed man in a white *guayabera*, his arms spread wide as if he longed to fly himself. They greeted him too, settling on his head, his chest, and even his nose, basking. He called them his darlings, his little voyagers, his angels, the souls of the dead returning home.

For as long as they stayed there was money in the village, as visitors came to marvel; their fluttering, gaudy life brought good luck. That luck did not last for him, despite worldwide attention. During a local festival he was killed and thrown in a holding pond, apparently, by illegal loggers who scorned and resented his guarding of the forest and the butterflies. Yet his friends might at least believe that his soul, too, would return in that gentle and benevolent form.

In the very old, soul and body seem already to be parting ways. My uncle's body, in his nineties and after a stroke, was gaunt and sinewy, with patchy discolourings and a suppurating wound on his elbow that would not heal. His hands were clumsy, and his mouth could not articulate words. But the usual boyish impishness danced in his eyes as he dabbed up biscuit crumbs or admired his favourite stick, a switch of hazel twined with an ivy stem. Looking at a woodcut of a hare, crouched, alert, he laughed with joy and tumbled out fast, indecipherable words. The spirit in him seemed to writhe and burn, impatient to be gone.

It is this that makes death most shocking, in my limited experience: less the gentle cessation of breath than the abrupt departure of fire. Life, I realised when my husband died, is of much more power and moment even than I had assumed. When Rumi writes that the Player's breath in the reed-flute is fire, it sounds like a poetic metaphor or a mode of action. But life is true fire: the heat we recognise on a cold day as our breath whitens round us and otherwise forget—until it leaves.

> The frail white petals I mistook for spring
> blown on the wind, darken the road below
> and prick my eyelids with a gravel sting,
> the kiss of snow.
>
> So memory nips again at that old place
> long-bandaged thick, and shiny new skin grown—
> how I, mistaken, kissed your just-dead face,
> as cold as stone.

Death may also intervene so suddenly that it seems a preposterous mistake. Surely life has merely paused; it must resume. As Shelley wrote, there is a spirit in us "at enmity with nothingness and dissolution."

Raoul Wallenberg was officially declared dead on October 26, 2016, and it was around that time that I wrote about him. Yet he had last been seen in 1945, surrounded by Soviet soldiers on his way to the Lubyanka prison in Moscow. He was carrying a briefcase. That case was full of blue-and-yellow "protection passes," a diplomat's bluff made "authentic" with Swedish government stamps and decorative Swedish crowns. With these he had saved the lives of thousands of Jews in Nazi-occupied Hungary in 1944, even kicking open the doors of cattle trucks bound for Auschwitz, under rifle fire, to hand his passes round. When he was arrested, he was on his way to succour more victims. Since no date for his death was ever given, those Wallenberg had rescued and their families felt he was still alive, haunting the streets and safe houses where he had paced unsleeping, with burning eyes, intent on saving as many as possible. To those who never saw him, he became a saviour-angel and a legend; he was surely one of the thirty-six "hidden saints" who helped persecuted Jews in each generation. Descendants of those who had been rescued still wanted to hug him and thank him, when he returned.

Those who later assumed he was dead put up memorials. But those, too, had a strangely impermanent look. They took the form of bronze briefcases, exact replicas of his own, with the initials "RW." One stood by the UN building in New York, one on the overgrown foundations of the house where he was born on Lidingö Island, near Stockholm. In Budapest one was left on a bench, as if at any moment he might come rushing back for it. His family went further: they kept his room ready for him, with fresh flowers, for the day he would come to the door, still dark-haired and middle-aged, with his briefcase in his hand.

Another of the missing, Keith Bennett, never saw middle age. He disappeared on Saddleworth Moor, a bleak expanse on the borders of Greater Manchester, on June 16, 1964, a victim of the child murderers Ian Brady and Myra Hindley. Almost every day until she died in 2012, his mother, Winnie Johnson, went up on the moor to look for him. She carried a spade, in case she found what might be a grave, and sometimes took his school photograph. It showed a nice lad with fair crew-cut hair and a cheeky grin, a boy who thought he could take care of himself but was, in fact, only just twelve, with a brand-new bike to prove it.

In the photo, Keith had his glasses on. When he went missing, he didn't. That might have been the problem: that he couldn't see that day, at any rate not well enough to get across the main Stockport road, which Winnie always worried about; or to notice the hard, evil eyes of the two people in the Mini Traveller that drew up beside him. He had cracked one of his lenses at swimming and hoped to get off school, but Winnie wasn't having any of that; she mended them with blue tape and put them ready for the next day. Once she had seen him safely over the zebra crossing, on the way to his gran's, and Keith had waved back, she felt that all was well.

But that wave was the last sign of the living boy. Winnie relived it every day. On Saddleworth she felt him close, so close that she sometimes took toys—a blue teddy bear, a cuddly dog—and hung them on a wire fence in the middle of nowhere, in case. Part of her was still ready to seize him by the hand and bring him home—home to where his glasses were mended and waiting, in a drawer in the back bedroom. The person she was looking for was still the Keith those glasses would fit, a right little dandy in his white zip-up jacket and black plastic shoes—the boy who, years after his disappearance, as she made the tea in the kitchen, had suddenly said, "Mam, I'm at the back of you."

When death happens inexplicably or too abruptly, those who are left cling all the more fiercely to continuing life. The man I saw sprawled on the southbound Victoria Line platform at Highbury and Islington was still running for the train, one arm stretched out and his legs askew, but stiffening, immobile. The platform was too narrow to stop and stare; two station staff put screens around him, but the rest of us pressed past, with work to do and appointments to keep, wrapping ourselves even tighter round life. At Benares, in India, a youth just knocked from his bicycle lay face-down in the road, the wheels of his bike continuing to turn, with the crowd already keeping back, out of respect, rather than running to help: already forming his funeral procession down to the Ganges and the ever-smouldering ghats.

In the same way, on that teeming lakeside beach at Levico Terme in the Dolomites, where the ambulance came screaming in to the boy pulled from the water, inert, his hair slicked like weed, and then did nothing for an hour, people returned to their sunbathing under the perfect sky. As for us, having sat awhile in the shadow of death, we moved to the beach next door where the news had not penetrated yet, and set up our chairs under the weeping willows. The safe water sparkled; the pedaloes ran to and fro. By three o'clock we were ready for an ice cream; the nougat was particularly good. And by four the Palm Court orchestra struck up its waltzes, old twirling with young, the alive and the possibly not-dead-at-all, down by the edge of the lake.

Each of those three had started the day buzzing with jobs and plans. The commuter would have brushed his shoes perhaps, knotted his tie (not that one, this one), pulled the creases out of his shirt. The mobile in his pocket would be crammed with messages, his head with tasks to remember (cancel X, Y's birthday, take car to service). The youth in Benares had picked a yellow shirt, perhaps his best, oiled his quiffed hair, which he was proud of, scooped dhal for breakfast from a tin bowl, pumped up his tyres to do his errands fast—too fast. The boy by the lake, as the papers told us the next day, had been on an outing with his mother and sister, not ideal company for a thirteen-year-old, and would have marvelled, as we all did, at the boys of his age and younger diving off the ten-metre board out in the deeper water. Every fibre of him would have wanted to do the same, and would have shrivelled at the thought of admitting, as was true, that he couldn't swim.

Details of this sort intensify the disbelief that, with one random act, all the inner complexity of life has been extinguished. That very complexity encourages the feeling that being persists, just as every sound and word ever uttered in a place sometimes seems to be carried in vibrations of the air. Those who were closest to me are still close, at my shoulder, with a gesture or a laugh or a piece of advice. This is more than memory; it is presence and communication or, in a word, *life*. In such encounters, death is not life's negation but a step to another stage.

But what if the act of self-expulsion is self-inflicted, and has thought—even desperate thought—behind it? Those are by far the hardest deaths to cover. Too often the reason for a suicide is unknown or is confused with accident; and the whole of the life is overshadowed by it. That motive may have been years growing, a hidden cancer behind a carefree mask, or it may have been a sudden impulse, or a dare. When Steve Fossett, setter of 116 land-and-sea records, flew his single-engine Bellanca Super Decathlon with no parachute over the Nevada sage-scrub and vanished, was it because he had become too old to break any more records? Was it miscalculation, or a wish to die doing what he most loved? When Steve Irwin, a cheeky Australian presenter of wildlife programmes, provoked a stingray just a bit more than necessary, was he pushing the extremes to make great television or had he meant to be more careful? Everyone saw him as a crazy, jokey bloke, but perhaps some darkness had inexplicably entered him. No one knew. Such deaths are reminders of how presumptuous my job is: how deep the mystery runs which, every week, I claim to have summed up in the compass of a page.

One such disappearance, however, had a calmer and gentler feel. It was that of Natalia Molchanova, "presumed drowned" in August 2015—whether by suicide or accident was never said. She could hold her breath underwater for nine minutes and, breath held, could swim horizontally for 237 metres or plunge down for 101, aided by a fin like a mermaid's tail. She would descend like a shining bead alongside a rope let down from the surface. Her diving suit, her own brand, was a mere 1.5 mm thick, thinner than fish-skin. Otherwise, she let the water clothe her. Every morsel

of energy and oxygen had to be conserved to penetrate the
depths of the sea. At the deepest point, her lungs would be
compressed to a quarter of their volume and would feel as if
no breath remained.

She was a daredevil on land, too, blonde, stocky, and
smiling as she roared around on motorbikes, but free-diving
was more than a dangerous sport to her. In order to do it
at all, she had to enter a different state, becoming one with
the serenity of the water. Her eyes would cease to focus on
particular objects; awareness shifted to the periphery of her
vision, and her heart and pulse rate slowed. She no longer felt
the panic of the almost-drowning, but had entered a state of
trance. Her poems described it:

> Unite in silence
> with the blue tender flow,
> and come to know
> your Spirit-law.

Natalia was one with creation then, in a sacred and prime-
val space. Her personality, however cheery and competitive,
could not get her back to the surface, she wrote; only her spirit
could. Possibly, on that last dive into the blue Mediterranean,
it felt no particular wish to.

Rumi, too, described this.

> Now your water-bead lets go
> and drops into the ocean,
> where it came from.

It no longer has the form it had,
but it's still water.
The essence is the same.

This giving up is not a repenting.
It's a deep honouring of yourself.

Natalia's death did not have the sting of a suicide. Her life seemed instead to have lost its limits, resolving fully into greater life. As she herself wrote:

I lost my body in the wave,
became instead its blue abyss.

Some think that Shelley, when he set out into a storm in 1822 in his flighty yacht *Ariel*, intended to do the same: to "solve the Great Mystery," as he put it once, by merging his boundless soul with the boundlessness of the sea. Like Natalia, he had longed for years to sink down in the lightest casing he had, the slightest shell, until he felt "his life beyond his limbs dilated" and there was no more limitation. Rumi would also say there was no more separation. The drop became the ocean, as the single note merged back into the singing reedbed of all created things. Being returned to being, breath to breath, which in truth had always been one.

Many do not hesitate to call this one force God, or Amun-Ra, or Brahman. But for the highest mystics it is a power even beyond the creator-deities, impossible (unlike those others) either to picture or to put into words. Both Rumi and Rilke avoided, as far as possible, giving it a name or any human quality. It was being itself, concealed within the dark, where perhaps it had been always: the only thing, from which everything flowed. Rumi, as usual, cut to the chase: "All that is, is love."

Dante, swept at last into Paradise, reached the same conclusion. He called the force he found there Love, for no other word could express the exhilarating power to which he was drawn close. The dazzling wheel of light he saw, the rotating cosmic machinery, was moved by something he could neither see nor describe: only adore, and only feel.

If it was love in operation here, as I would like to believe—if it is love that fills and charges us—it is not obviously the kind that humans usually understand. Lives are often too desperate, cruel, and inexplicable—even without the tendency of humans to mess up their own affairs—to be credited to an act of divine affection. But affection seems too emotional a thought. This is love that rolls on regardless, according to its own laws. Instead of pausing over our troubles, it pours itself out continually among them, not remote but near, as near as our jugular vein. It is the love between iron and a magnet, or between tides and the moon: love as intrinsic to the universe as electromagnetic force. Overwhelming, undiscriminating, necessary love, as even I had sensed it in the lilac and the blackthorn trees. Love given, taken, returned, love seeking what it does not have: the simplest thing. On second thought, perhaps it is not so far removed from the love we already know and sometimes think divine.

And there is nothing, no space, that is not filled with this. Even the silty depths of a lake near Peterborough, and the trembling rod above, and the fish that rises like a lazy twist of gold to be caught, and let go, and caught again.

Obituary Subjects in Order of Appearance (with *Economist* issue date)

Margaret Gelling, place-name expert	5/14/2009
Cedric Robinson, guide to the Morecambe Bay sands	
(written as a Christmas spare and unpublished)	
Marie Smith, last speaker of Eyak	2/7/2008
Dr. G. Yunupingu, Aboriginal singer	8/5/2017
Li Wenliang, ophthalmologist of Wuhan	2/15/2020
Luciano Pavarotti, tenor	9/13/2007
Joan Sutherland, *prima donna assoluta*	10/30/2010
Miriam Makeba, singer of South Africa	11/13/2008
Steven Weinberg, theoretical physicist	7/31/2021
James Lovelock, author of the Gaia hypothesis	8/3/2022
Shirley Temple, child star	2/15/2014
Irving Milchberg, scamp of the Warsaw ghetto	2/22/2014
Qusai Abtini, child star of Aleppo	8/13/2016
Seamus Heaney, poet of Ireland	9/5/2013
Eavan Boland, poet of women's Ireland	5/16/2020
Derek Walcott, poet of St. Lucia	4/1/2017
Stanley Kunitz, poet of New England	5/27/2006
Les Murray, poet of Australia	5/11/2019
Tim Samaras, tornado tracker	6/15/2013
Brother Roger, founder of Taizé	8/27/2005
Baba Amte, champion of India's lepers	3/1/2008
Aretha Franklin, soul singer	8/25/2018
Bip, a figure of mime	9/29/2007
Johnny Kingdom, gravedigger	
and nature photographer	9/22/2018
Homero Gómez, protector of monarch butterflies	2/8/2020
Raoul Wallenberg, saviour of	
the Jews of Budapest	11/12/2016

Winnie Johnson, searching mother   8/25/2012
Natalia Molchanova, free-diver   8/15/2015

With warm thanks to Zanny Minton Beddoes, editor of the *Economist*, for allowing the use of these obituaries or paraphrases of them.

References for Quoted Works

I: Outbreath

1: Possessing

6 **Paul Valéry's words, "*toujours recommencée*"**: Paul Valéry, "Le Cimetière Marin," verse 1, line 4.

15 **Aubrey's observations**: John Aubrey, *Brief Lives* (London: Vintage, 2016): Bushell, p. 42; Bacon, p. 9; Hobbes, p. 150; Harrington, p. 126; Oughtred, pp. 222–3.

15 **Suetonius**: Gaius Suetonius Tranquillus, *The Twelve Caesars*, trans. Robert Graves (London: Penguin, 1989): Augustus on boxing, p. 81; "My Lord," p. 84; asparagus, p. 101; Tiberius's half-eaten dishes, p. 132; the Sirens' song, p. 149; Claudius at dice, p. 209.

18 **"Two bags of grass"**: Hunter S. Thompson, *Fear and Loathing in Las Vegas* Second Vintage Books Edition (New York: Vintage Books, 1998), p. 4.

2: Seizing

28 **Eliot, "unheard music"**: T. S. Eliot, "Burnt Norton," in *Four Quartets*, I, line 27.

28 **"Go, go, go"**: Eliot, "Burnt Norton," I, lines 42–3.

30 **Beckett, "Siege laid again . . ."**: Taken from the photograph of the handwritten and typed original in Anne Atik, *How It Was: A Memoir of Samuel Beckett*, 1st. ed (Emeryville, CA: Shoemaker Hoard, 2005), plate 15, p. 32.

31 **"volatil Hermes"**: Milton, *Paradise Lost*, bk. 3, line 603.

31 **"like a seagull catching fish"**: Homer, *The Odyssey*, trans. Emily Wilson (New York: W. W. Norton, 2018), bk. 5, lines 51–3.

34 **"Between the idea"**: T. S. Eliot, "The Hollow Men," V, lines 5–9.

35 **"An invisible bird"**: Rumi, "Where Are We?" in *Selected Poems of Rumi*, trans. Coleman Barks (London: Penguin, 1999), p. 15, lines 1–5.

42 **A sparrow flying**: Bede, *Ecclesiastical History of England*, bk. 2, chap. 13.

50 **"We have all of us . . ."**: William Wordsworth, "The Old Cumberland Beggar," line 153.

50 **"One Love"**: "One Love," songwriters Bob Marley and Curtis Mayfield, track 5 on Bob Marley and the Wailers, *Exodus*, Island, 1977, 33⅓ rpm.

3: Indwelling

66 **"Low breathings"**: William Wordsworth, *The Prelude: Or Growth of a Poet's Mind* (1850 text), bk. 1, lines 330–32.

67 **"As if with voluntary power"**: Wordsworth, *The Prelude*, book 1, lines 379–85.

67 **"To every natural form"**: Wordsworth, *The Prelude*, bk. 3, lines 131–36.

67 **"sentiment of Being"**: Wordsworth, *The Prelude*, bk. 2, lines 400–405.

74 **"nearer than your jugular vein"**: Rumi, "There Is a Tall Tower That Love Builds," in *Like This: Rumi, 43 Odes*, trans. Coleman Barks (Johnson City, TN: Maypop, 1990).

4: Returning

77 **Lorca's agonised lament:** Federico García Lorca, "Llanto por Ignacio Sánchez Mejías," 2; "La Sangre Derramada," last section.

81 **"A presence that disturbs me":** William Wordsworth, "Lines Composed a Few Miles Above Tintern Abbey," July 13, 1798, lines 93–102.

86 **"God picks up the reed-flute":** Rumi, "Each Note," in *Selected Poems of Rumi*, trans. Coleman Barks, pp. 102–3, lines 24–31.

88 **Wisdom:** Proverbs 8:22–31; Ecclesiasticus XXIV, passim.

89 **"A wealth you cannot":** Rumi, "#52: The Only Obligation," *Rumi: Bridge to the Soul: Journeys into the Music and Silence of the Heart*, trans. Coleman Barks (New York: HarperOne, 2007), p. 130.

89 **Adam waking:** Milton, *Paradise Lost*, bk. 5, lines 185–91.

90 **"I will sing to the Lord":** Psalm 104:33 (author's paraphrase).

90 **"It is folly":** "119: The Praises of God," in Kenneth Hurlstone Jackson, *A Celtic Miscellany: Translations from the Celtic Literature* (London: Penguin Classics, 1977), p. 136.

96 **"God possesses . . .":** William Butler Yeats, "A Visionary," from *The Collected Works of William Butler Yeats*, vol. 5, The Celtic Twilight and Stories of Red Hanrahan, e-book #49612 (Project Gutenburg e-books, 2015), https://www.gutenberg.org/files/59768/59768-h /59768-h.htm, p. 11.

97 **"dark / and like a web":** Rainer Maria Rilke, *Prayers of a Young Poet: The Book of Hours*, trans. Mark S. Burrows (Brewster, MA: Paraclete Press, 2013), poem I. 3.

97 **"mining the silences":** Rilke, *Prayers of a Young Poet*, poem I. 16.

97 **"a great presence stirring":** Rilke, *Rilke's Book of Hours: Love Poems to God*, trans. Anita Barrows and Joanna Macy (New York: Riverhead Books, 2005), p. 63.

97 **"the drifting mist that":** Rilke, *Prayers of a Young Poet*, poem I. 4.

97 **"I've been circling . . .":** Rilke (from *The Book of Hours*), *A Year with Rilke: Daily Readings from the Best of Rainer Maria Rilke*, trans. and ed. Joanna Macy and Anita Barrows (New York: HarperOne, 2009), p. 122 (May 2), 5–8.

100 Ch'eng-kung Sui, "The secluded gentleman . . .": Douglas A.
     White, "Cheng-kung Sui's Poetic Essay on Whistling, the Hsiao
     Fu," (Cambridge, MA: Harvard University, 1994), 429–33 passim;
     Wikipedia, s.v. "Transcendental Whistling," accessed May 22, 2024,
     https://en.wikipedia.org/wiki/Transcendental_whistling.

100 "Be that empty": Rumi, "The Reed Flute's Song," *Selected Poems of
     Rumi*, p. 18.

II: Inbreath

1: Possessing

105 "What is life?": Percy Shelley, "On Life," in *The Prose Works of
     Percy Bysshe Shelley*, ed. H. Buxton Forman, vol. 2. (London, 1880),
     pp. 257–61.

107 James Lovelock's most famous hypothesis: James Lovelock, *Gaia: A
     New Look at Life on Earth*, 2nd ed. (Oxford: Oxford University
     Press, 2016), especially pp. 4, 13, 135.

109 "unusually intense and vivid": Shelley, "On Life," *The Prose Works*,
     p. 261.

109 Wordsworth, in his "Immortality Ode": William Wordsworth,
     "Ode: Intimations of Immortality from Recollections of Early
     Childhood," VII, 86; VIII, 111, 123.

112 "I saw one life": William Wordsworth, *The Prelude* (1805–6
     version), bk. 2, line 430.

112 old Kentish: W. D. Parish, *A Dictionary of the Kentish Dialect* (East
     Sussex: Farncombe, 1888), passim.

2: Seizing

129 "with an eye . . .": William Wordsworth, "Lines Composed a Few
     Miles Above Tintern Abbey," July 13, 1798, lines 47–49.

129 **"serene and blessed"**: Wordsworth, "Lines Composed a Few Miles," lines 41, 45–46.

129 **"Flower in the crannied wall"**: Alfred Tennyson, "Flower in the Crannied Wall," 1863.

130 **Coleridge had done the same**: Samuel Taylor Coleridge, *Coleridge's Notebooks: A Selection*, ed. Seamus Perry (Oxford: Oxford University Press, 2002), p. 1, no. 2.

130 **"Riveted steel . . ."**: Seamus Heaney, "The Pitchfork," in *Seeing Things* (London: Faber, 1991), p. 23, lines 9–12.

130 **"saying *hush*"**: Heaney, "The Pulse," (in "Three Drawings," 2), *Seeing Things*, p. 13, lines 1–3.

130 **"so unanswerably landed"**: Seamus Heaney, "A Shiver," in *District and Circle* (London: Faber, 2006).

131 **"sump and seedbed"**: Seamus Heaney, "Kinship," in *North* (London: Faber, 1975), iv, 3.

131 **"spilled their heavy lip"**: Seamus Heaney, "Churning Day," in *Death of a Naturalist* (London: Faber, 1966), p. 11, lines 10–11.

131 **"cargoed with"**: Heaney, "The Settle Bed," *Seeing Things*, p. 28, line 18.

131 **fresh-sawn boards**: Heaney, "Markings," *Seeing Things*, pp. 8–9, II, 2.

131 **"on the scene"**: Eavan Boland, "It's a Woman's World," *New Collected Poems* (Manchester: Carcanet, 2005), p. 111.

131 **"smooth / Mimicry"**: Boland "Code," 1; "Marriage," 4.

131 **"and in its own Mineral curve"**: Ibid., 5.

132 **"leaping the breakers"**: Derek Walcott, *Omeros* (London: Faber, 1990), XXIV, 130–31.

132 **egret as pen**: Walcott, "White Egrets," in *White Egrets* (London: Faber, 2010).

132 **"obliquity burrowing"**: Walcott, "The Castaway," *Collected Poems, 1948-1984* (New York: Farrar, Straus, and Giroux, 1986), 3-4.

132 **"towards the white noise . . ."**: Walcott, *Omeros*, LXVIII, 241.

132 **"stretched into bird"**: Stanley Kunitz, "Father and Son," in *The Poems of Stanley Kunitz, 1928–1978* (Boston: Atlantic / Little Brown, 1979).

133 **"tried to loop me home"**: Kunitz, "The Testing Tree," in *The Wild Braid: A Poet Reflects on a Century in the Garden* (New York: W. W. Norton, 2005), 33.

133 **"nosing upstream"**: Kunitz, "King of the River," from *Passing Through: The Later Poems, New and Selected* (New York: W. W. Norton, 1995), 6–10.

133 **"Becoming, never being"**: Kunitz, "Change," in *The Poems of Stanley Kunitz.*

134 **"curveting, fish-leaping"**: Les Murray, "Walking to the Cattle Place," in *New Collected Poems* (Manchester: Carcanet, 1991), "5. Death Words."

134 **"puffed felt"**: Les Murray, "Spurwing Plover," in *Ethnic Radio: Poems by Les Murray* (Sydney: Angus & Robertson, 1977).

134 **"thin with frosted straw"**: Les Murray, "Hayfork Point," in *New Collected Poems*, p. 33.

134 **"decaying / to slatternly paper"**: "SMLE," st. 1, *New Collected Poems*, p. 49.

134 **cockspur bush, "sharp-thorned"**: Les Murray, "Cockspur Bush," Best Poems Encyclopedia, accessed May 22, 2024, https:// www.best-poems.net/les_murray/cockspur_bush.html, lines 4–5.

134 **"the interiors"**: Federico Lorca, *Impresiones y Paisajes* (Madrid: Ediciones Catedra, 1993), prologue.

134 **Rilke, too, in his *New Poems***: Rainer Rilke, *Neue Gedichte/New Poems*, trans. Stephen Cohn (Manchester: Carcanet, 2004), "Panther," p. 61; "Ancient Torso of Apollo," p. 143.

135 **"the world outside"**: Rilke, "Bowl of Roses III," *New Poems*, p. 139.

139 **"list"**: W. D. Parish, *A Dictionary of the Kentish Dialect* (East Sussex: Farncombe, 1888), passim.

142 **Coleridge and starlings:** Samuel Coleridge, *The Notebooks of Samuel Taylor Coleridge*, ed. Kathleen Coburn, vol. 1 (New York: Pantheon for Bollinger Foundation, 1957), no. 582.

143 **"There are only two great and related"**: Rainer Rilke, entry in the Schmargendorf diary for April 7, 1900; see *Diaries of a Young Poet*, trans. Edward Snow and Michael Winkler (W.W. Norton, 1998), p. 131.

143 **Aubrey noted that Francis Bacon:** John Aubrey, *Brief Lives* (London: Vintage, 2016), p. 16.

143 **Bashō on the spirits that drove him:** Matsuo Bashō, *The Narrow Road to the Deep North and Other Travel Sketches*, trans. Nobuyuki Yuasa (London: Penguin Classics, 1966), p. 97.

144 **The sight of an abandoned sheepfold:** the William Wordsworth poems referred to in this paragraph are, in order, "Michael," "I Wandered Lonely as a Cloud," and "Ode: Intimations of Immortality," IV, pp. 55–58.

144 **"when you and the object":** Bashō, *Narrow Road*, p. 33.

145 **pines of Matsushima:** Bashō, pp. 115–16.

145 **"Touch the cloth":** Rumi, "#8," *Rumi: Bridge to the Soul: Journeys into the Music and Silence of the Heart*, trans. Coleman Barks (New York: HarperOne, 2007), 2–3, 4–6, 8–9, 13–14.

146 **"Let that [invisible] musician":** Rumi, "On Silence," in *Selected Poems of Rumi*, trans. Coleman Barks, p. 17.

146 **"following the love":** Rumi, "Love for Certain Work," trans. Coleman Barks, Rumi Days, July 19, 2010, http://rumidays .blogspot.com/2010/07/love-for-certain-work.html.

149 **Wordsworth longed, when skating:** William Wordsworth, *Prelude*, I, 453.

149 **children in the wind:** Coleridge, *Notebooks of Coleridge*, vol. 1, no. 330 (14).

153 **"whirled about without a center":** Coleridge, *Notebooks of Coleridge*, vol. 3 (Princeton, NJ: Princeton University Press, 1973), no. 3999.

3: Indwelling

163 **"Our birth is but":** William Wordsworth, "Ode: Intimations of Immortality from Recollections of Early Childhood," V, 59–66.

166 **Plato's soul:** Plato, *Phaedrus*, 25.

167 **"hushed casket":** John Keats, "To Sleep," line 14.

167 **"secret heart-house"**: Rumi, "#52: The Only Obligation," *Rumi: Bridge to the Soul: Journeys into the Music and Silence of the Heart*, trans. Coleman Barks (New York: HarperOne, 2007), p. 130.

167 **"the secret place of the heart"**: Mundaka Upanishad, in *The Upanishads* [selections], trans. Juan Mascaró (London: Penguin, 1965), chap. 2, p. 78.

169 **"What cannot be spoken"**: Kena Upanishad, *Upanishads*, part 1, p. 51.

170 **"He who abides in Me"**: John 15:5 (author paraphrase).

170 **"There are diversities"**: 1 Corinthians 12:6 KJV.

170 **"The breath of life is one"**: Kaushitaki Upanishad, *Upanishads*, part 3, vv. 2–3, p. 106.

170 **"I looked for myself"**: Rumi, "The Beloved," in *Rumi: The Book of Love: Poems of Ecstasy and Longing*, trans. Coleman Barks (San Francisco: HarperOne, 2005).

171 **Dante began to sense**: Dante Alighieri, *The Divine Comedy*, I, "Inferno," canto XXIV, 58–60.

172 **"Stay with me"**: © 1984, Ateliers et Presses de Taizé, 71250, Taizé, France

172 **"memory of music fled"**: Percy Shelley, "Hymn to Intellectual Beauty," v. 1, line 10.

177 **"A silent, fragile hand"**: "The Third Eye" ("Le Troisième Oeil"), 1981, courtesy of Gemini Gallery: moicani.over-blog.com /article-31846858.html.

4: Returning

179 **"Man that is born"**: Henry Purcell, "Funeral Sentences," based on Job 14:1–2, Emmanuel Music, accessed May 22, 2024, https:// www.emmanuelmusic.org/other-translations/purcell-funeral -sentences-for-queen-mary.

184 **"at enmity with nothingness"**: Percy Shelley, "On Life," in *The Prose Works of Percy Bysshe Shelley*, ed. H. Buxton Forman, vol. 2, (London, 1880), p. 260.

190 **"Unite in silence"**: Natalia Molchanova, poem translated by Mikhail Soldatov, in "The deepest dive (Obituary: Natalia Molchanova)," *GeoGarage blog,* August 15, 2015, https://blog.geogarage.com/2015_08_09_archive.html.

190 **"Now your water-bead"**: Rumi, "The Seed Market," in *Selected Poems of Rumi*, trans. Coleman Barks (London: Penguin, 1999), 13–20, pp. 153–55.

191 **"I lost my body"**: Molchanova, "The Depth," lines 8, 11, in Justin Housman, "Natalia Molchanova, World's Best Free Diver, Vanished During Final Dive," March 1, 2024, https://www.adventure-journal.com/2024/03/natalia-molchanova-world-s-best-free-diver-vanished-during-final-dive/.

191 **"solve the Great Mystery"**: Edward John Trelawny, *The Last Days of Shelley and Byron*, ed. J. E. Morpurgo (London: Folio Society, 1952), pp. 155–61.

191 **"his life beyond his limbs"**: Percy Shelley, "Marengh," XXIII, 130–35.

192 **"All that is"**: Rumi, "#76," *Rumi: Bridge to the Soul: Journeys into the Music and Silence of the Heart*, trans. Coleman Barks (New York: HarperOne, 2007).

192 **Dante, swept at last:** Dante, *The Divine Comedy*, III, "Paradiso," XXXIII, 144–45.

Acknowledgments

THIS BOOK COULD NOT HAVE BEEN WRITTEN WITH-
out the courage of Bill Emmott, then editor of the *Economist*,
to let me loose on the Obituary section (which he had intro-
duced to the paper), and the constant kind indulgence of the
editors who followed him, John Micklethwait and Zanny
Minton Beddoes. I have been given virtually free rein, even
when I wanted to write about almost unknown people, or
indeed about fish. I am grateful, too, to Keith Colquhoun,
my predecessor in the job, who set an example of choosing
unusual subjects and sometimes treating them in startling
ways. My years of doing the Obituaries (almost half my
sojourn at the paper) have been the most satisfying I have
ever spent there, in a place where I don't believe I have ever
spent a tedious day.

The first version of this book, however, was not built
around the Obituaries and was conceived entirely as poetry.
Three particular friends, Peter Abbs, Lisa Dart, and Nomi
Rowe, read the first version and managed simultaneously to
encourage me and to advise a different path. Another friend

heroically read both versions, again dispensing encourage-
ment and wise advice, as indeed did my agent, Andrew
Wylie, and my editor at Cape, Bea Hemming. If anyone
put the germ of "life stories" into my head, it was probably
Bea—who deserves thanks both for that and for tolerating
my eccentric ways of working, refined for years under Dan
Franklin, whereby the manuscript just appears on the editor's
desk with no notice of subject, synopsis, or anything else, and
on a totally random topic.

Also at Cape, thanks are owed to Graeme Hall, who
organised the schedule both efficiently and kindly; Mandy
Greenfield, my eagle-eyed and most understanding copy edi-
tor; John Garrett, who assiduously proofread; Clara Irvine,
who tirelessly tracked down all the permissions; and to
Anneka Sandher, for designing the beautiful cover.

Lastly, I would like to doff my cap to the wonderful
Research Department at the *Economist*, who have put up
over the years with a deluge of obscure sources and inex-
pert online hyperlinks and have set me straight with infinite
patience. Any mistakes in the text are highly unlikely to be
in the Obituary sections, and will be my own. The opinions
and the conclusion, though shared with many greater seekers,
are also my own.

Ann Wroe

Permissions

THANKS ARE DUE TO THE FOLLOWING PUBLISHERS for kind permission to reproduce copyrighted material.

Ateliers et Presses de Taizé for Taizé chant © Ateliers et Presses de Taizé, 71250 Taizé, France.

Carcanet Press for *New Collected Poems* by Eavan Boland; *New Collected Poems* by Les Murray; and *Neue Gedichte/New Poems* by Rainer Maria Rilke, translated by Stephen Cohn.

Faber & Faber Ltd for *How It Was: A Memoir of Samuel Beckett* by Anne Atik; *Four Quartets* and *The Poems of T. S. Eliot Volume I* by T. S. Eliot; and *Omeros* by Derek Walcott.

HarperCollins Publishers Ltd for *Rumi: Bridge to the Soul: Journeys into the Music and Silence of the Heart* © 2007 Rumi, Coleman Barks; and *A Year with Rilke: Daily Readings from the Best of Rainer Maria Rilke*, translated and edited by Joanna Macy and Anita Barrows, © Joanna Macy and Anita Barrows, 2009.

Little, Brown & Co for "Change" from *The Poems of Stanley Kunitz, 1928–1978* by Stanley Kunitz.

Paraclete Press for *Prayers of a Young Poet* by Rainer

Maria Rilke, translated by Mark S. Burrows © 2016. English translation by Mark S. Burrows.

Penguin Books Ltd for "Ich lebe mein Leben . . ."/"I live my life in widening" by Rainer Maria Rilke, © 1996 by Anita Barrows and Joanna Macy, from *Rilke's Book of Hours: Love Poems to God* by Rainer Maria Rilke, translated by Anita Barrows and Joanna Macy, used by permission of Riverhead, an imprint of Penguin Publishing Group, a division of Penguin Random House LLC. All rights reserved; *Selected Poems of Rumi*, translation © Coleman Barks, 1999; *The Twelve Caesars* by Suetonius, translation © Robert Graves, 1989; *The Bhagavad Gita*, translated by Juan Mascaró, published by Penguin Classics. Translation © Juan Mascaró, 1962; *The Upanishads*, translated by Juan Mascaró, published by Penguin Classics. Translation © Juan Mascaró, 1965; and *The Narrow Road to the Deep North and Other Travel Sketches* by Matsuo Bashō, translated by Nobuyuki Yuasa, published by Penguin Classics. Copyright © Nobuyuki Yuasa, 1966.

Taylor & Francis Group for *A Celtic Miscellany: Translations from the Celtic Literature* by Kenneth Hurlstone Jackson, copyright (1951) Penguin Classics.

W. W. Norton for "King of the River," from *Passing Through: The Later Poems New and Selected* by Stanley Kunitz. Copyright © 1995 by Stanley Kunitz. Used by permission of W. W. Norton & Company, Inc; and *The Schmargendorf Diary* in *Diaries of a Young Poet* by Rainer Maria Rilke, translated by Edward Snow and Michael Winkler.

Every effort has been made to contact all copyright holders. The publisher will be pleased to amend in future editions any errors or omissions brought to their attention.